# The
# Rights of Women

HAYDEN
AMERICAN
VALUES SERIES:
*Challenges & Choices*

JACK NELSON, *Series Editor*

*Department of Science and Humanities Education*
*Rutgers University*

THE RIGHTS OF WOMEN
Sylvia Feldman
THE ENVIRONMENT: A Human Crisis
Michael Piburn
DISSENT AND PROTEST
David Naylor
CITY LIFE
William Lowe
WAR AND WAR PREVENTION
Joseph Moore & Roberta Moore
THE POOR
Kenneth Carlson
URBAN GROWTH
Robert Torrone & Paul Wilhelm

# The
# Rights of Women

**SYLVIA FELDMAN**

## HAYDEN BOOK COMPANY, INC.
Rochelle Park, New Jersey

*For Mervyn and Harriet*

*Library of Congress Cataloging in Publication Data*

Feldman, Sylvia D
    The rights of women.

    (Hayden American values series)
    1. Women in the United States. 2. Woman—
History and condition of women. I. Title.
HQ1420.F37        301.41'2'0973        73-11929
ISBN 0-8104-5901-9

1    2    3    4    5    6    7    8    9    PRINTING

74  75  76  77  78  79  80  81  82    YEAR

*Design* A. Victor Schwarz
*Editorial* S. W. Cook
*Production* Helen L. Garfinkle
*Consultant* Dr. Abraham Resnick

# Editor's Introduction

How old will you be in the year 2000?
How will the world be different?
If you could choose, what things would you change between now and then?
What would you want to leave unchanged?

Social problems such as discrimination, pollution, crime, and poverty are the result of decisions made in the past. Are there solutions for these and other problems? Will they have changed by the year 2000?

What new challenges are likely to develop?
What choices are now available?

America shares a dominant value with many parts of the world—the idea of a democratic society based on human rights and social justice. This is not always achieved, and there are many disputes over how it can be achieved, but basic documents like the Declaration of Independence and the Constitution express the strong belief that this value is worth the struggle against repression, ignorance, and intolerance. A democratic society depends upon thoughtful and enlightened citizens. The challenges of social issues demand critical inquiry. The choices involve consequences for the future.

The HAYDEN AMERICAN VALUES SERIES: CHALLENGES AND CHOICES presents social issues in contemporary society. This book provides a framework for examining one of these issues. A similar format is found in each book. Each includes:

- Case studies illustrating the issue by focusing on human situations.
- Factual information about the issue which can be used as evidence in making social decisions.
- Divergent views and opposing value judgments showing a variety of values involved in solving the issue.
- Futuristic scenarios illustrating possible consequences of social decisions in future human situations.
- Suggestions for involvement in the issues and the decisions.
- Recommendations for further study.

J. N.

# Acknowledgments

I wish to thank Starry Kreuger, who generously provided me with numerous materials and suggestions.

My sincere appreciation to the Women's Center of New York City, the New York Chapter of NOW (National Organization for Women), and the Women's Bureau, United States Department of Labor, for their help in preparing this book.

S. F.

# Contents

# Before You Begin

Studying the problem of women's role in society means re-considering one's attitudes about both men and women. Before you begin, you may want to take the following quiz.

On a separate sheet of paper, copy the headings given below. For each, make up a list of ten descriptive adjectives, such as, for example, "wise," "generous," "kind," and "emotional." Don't think too long about any one adjective, and don't worry about what you ought to say. Be honest, putting down exactly what you feel.

| A *man should be*: | A *woman should be*: |
|---|---|
| 1. | 1. |
| 2. | 2. |
| 3. | 3. |
| 4. | 4. |
| 5. | 5. |
| 6. | 6. |
| 7. | 7. |
| 8. | 8. |
| 9. | 9. |
| 10. | 10. |

After you have finished the lists, ask yourself these questions:

- What do the lists have in common?
- Did I describe men and women in opposite terms?
- Why did I describe them as I did?

Save the lists. Then, after you have finished this book, look at them again and ask yourself these questions:

- How would I change them? Why?
- Have my attitudes changed? How? Why?

# Chapter 1

# Three Women at Crisis

These are the stories of Joyce, Thelma, and Rita. The problems they face are shared by a large number of women. You can see them on television or read about them daily in newspapers and magazines. They have formed the basis of numerous sociological, psychological, and statistical studies.

As you read their stories, try to consider the world from their point of view. Try to understand them—not only where they are, but how they came to be there. Decide what you think they should do, what seems right for them.

## Joyce: Being a Housewife

Joyce realized that she was bored at 10:52 A.M. She remembered the time distinctly. She was sitting in the kitchen, having her fourth cup of coffee, feeling so tired that she had to force herself to stay awake so that she wouldn't go upstairs and lie down until Amy came home from nursery school.

"I've got too much to do," she said to herself. "I've just got too much to do."

The morning had begun like any other. Up at 6:00 A.M., she quickly combed her hair, called Tom, her husband, and went into the kitchen to make breakfast. Joyce believed in breakfast because her mother had taught her that "a man must have a good meal in the morning. He's the provider; he needs his strength." So for sixteen years she had gotten up and made Tom breakfast —orange juice, two eggs, bacon, toast, and coffee. Since he had to catch the 7:15 bus into the city, Tom showered quickly, dressed, ate, and skimmed the front page of the paper. They said "Good morning" to each other, but, otherwise, rarely spoke. Joyce knew that from the moment he awakened, Tom was already thinking about work so that by the time he came into the kitchen, he had left for the day, his mind and heart being now at the office, not here with her and the children.

They sat at the table together, Joyce drinking her first cup of coffee but not eating. "It's too early to eat," she thought to herself. She sat across the table from Tom and smiled, trying not to look tired. "A good wife gets up and sees her husband off to work," her mother had told her. So everyday she sat with Tom, watching him eat. When it was time for him to leave, she walked him to the door, carrying his briefcase. He gave her a peck on the cheek and left.

Since it was too early to awaken the children, she always returned to the kitchen, set the oven timer, poured herself another cup of coffee, and waited for fifteen minutes. She kept looking at the clock because she knew she had to keep on schedule or the children would be late for school. She sat, her eyes wide, half sleeping, half dreaming, until the timer buzzed. Up again, she went first to wake Kate, who at thirteen stayed the longest in the bathroom. Next she called Stevie, who at the age of ten dressed carelessly but quickly, ran downstairs two at a time, gulped a glass of milk, and was off.

Joyce barely spoke to the older children in the morning. They were so independent that they really didn't need her. They could take care of themselves. Sometimes she felt she was merely a traffic manager, whose functions were to make certain that Kate was out of the bathroom so Stevie could get in, that glasses of milk were on the table as they rushed by, that the schoolbooks were collected so no time would be wasted looking for them.

It was a pleasure to wake Amy, who was only four. Amy was always so happy to see her. "Good morning, love," Joyce would say, and Amy would grab her, hugging her tightly for a moment. She and Amy chatted about what to wear to school.

"I want the yellow one."

"But, honey, it's dirty."

"But I want it!"

"It's in the laundry. How about the blue shirt instead? Look at the pretty daisy on it. You always liked that. I'll wash the yellow shirt today, and you can wear it to school tomorrow. I promise."

"Oh, all right."

They chatted, too, about nursery school,—"Mommy, do you know what Tommy did . . . ?" and about breakfast.

"Honey, you have to eat your cereal. It's your favorite, and it's good for you."

"But I don't want to."

"You have to."

"Oh, well, okay."

They talked until Amy's ride came. Joyce always walked her to the car, gave her a hug, and said, "I'll see you at 12:30. Have a good time, love." She waved goodbye and walked back to the house.

It was 9:15 A.M. She was alone.

Joyce went into the kitchen, rinsed the breakfast dishes, and put them in the dishwasher. She set a place for herself at the table, made a soft boiled egg and toast, and ate. Usually, she ate quickly because she was worried about finishing the chores— making the beds, dusting, vacuuming the living room—before Amy returned.

But this morning was different. She sat, just sat, thinking, feeling slightly depressed and very tired. She had another cup of coffee. She knew she ought to begin, but she couldn't. She looked at the clock, watched the second hand move slowly around. "I've got to get busy," she thought. But she continued to sit.

"I'm bored," she said to herself. Out of habit, she looked at the clock. It was 10:52 A.M. "What am I going to do with myself? Here I am, thirty-seven, and all I do is clean house, and cook, and clean, and take care of children, and clean, and cook, and shop.

"But you love Tom, don't you?" she asked herself. "Of course, I do. After sixteen years of marriage, I still do, maybe even more than I did when we were younger. I know he's a good man, a man who loves his family. And he has always been so good to me. When we were struggling, he never thought of himself. Everything he earned went to the family. I still remember that beautiful silk dress he gave me for Christmas. How long ago was that? Oh, yes, it must be about thirteen years now. To have spent a hundred dollars on a dress! Tom, who hadn't had a new suit in two years, spent all that money on me because he wanted me to 'think beautiful.'

"He really wanted to live nearer work. It's because of me that we're way out here, because of me that he has to travel an hour each way. But I wanted the children to have space and a nice house. I wanted them to be able to play in fields, not on concrete, to live in a nice area, to go to good schools.

"They all have lives of their own—Tom and the children. I'm just an appendage. And the children are growing up. Even Amy won't need me very much in a few years. Sometimes I feel so lost, as though I don't know who I am anymore. I'm just Tom's wife, or Stevie's mother, or the lady who drives the car pool.

"I'm not anybody, not anybody myself," she thought and felt frightened. "I'll call Betty." She got up quickly and dialed. Betty came over almost immediately. They had coffee and gossiped. After a while, Joyce tried to explain how she felt.

"Oh, sure," Betty laughed. "I feel that way often. It's nothing to worry about; the routine is just getting you down. You need a vacation. Maybe you and Tom should get away for a few days, just the two of you. Hank and I did it last year. We had a great time.

"You know I felt exactly the way you do now a few months after Paul's birth. I was really depressed, let me tell you. I didn't want to do anything but sleep. I couldn't get up in the morning, and I was so nervous that I was always screaming at Hank and the kids. Hank got so worried that he took me to a doctor who prescribed some tranquilizers. They helped a lot, they really did. And the doctor gave me some good advice, too. He told me not to be so conscientious. He said, 'So what if you don't dust everyday. The world won't come to an end.'

"Do you know what I do when I feel depressed? I hire a baby-sitter to be in the house when the children come home from school. And I get all dressed up. I go into the city, treat myself to a fancy lunch, and find the saddest movie in town. I buy a big bag of candy, and I sit in that dark movie house, all alone, eating it, and having a good cry. It works wonders. Afterwards, I feel drained and at peace.

"Sometimes, if I'm in the mood, I go shopping, buying myself the prettiest thing I can find. Don't tell Hank about that, please. He doesn't know. I pretend I've had the things for a long time. Once in a while, I have my hair done. Looking pretty makes me like myself better.

"What you're feeling is perfectly normal. Don't worry about it. Hey, I hear a car. I guess Amy's back."

"Oh, dear, I've got to fix lunch. Stay and eat with us."

"No, thanks. I can't. Grocery shopping today."

Joyce felt reassured after talking to Betty. She had a good afternoon with Amy, the two of them wandering around the shopping center, looking in the shop windows, and buying ice cream cones.

But the mood returned the next day. She felt depressed and restless. Which was why she went to the rap session.

Sherry, a neighbor she knew only slightly, called and invited her. "It's a meeting sponsored by a women's group called NOW, the National Organization for Women. They hold rap sessions once a month. This month's one is being held in the high school because they're trying to organize a chapter here. Do come. You'll find it interesting."

Thursday night Sherry picked her up in a car and they drove the three-minute ride to the school.

"It should be fun," Sherry said.

"Who'll be there? Anyone I know?" Joyce asked.

"I'm not sure. Each of us invited ten others, and we tried to canvass the area, including the apartments. I'm curious, too."

About seventy women came. A few Joyce knew or had seen frequently enough in the shopping center to feel that she knew them slightly. Groups of ten were formed, and by chance Joyce was placed in a group where she knew no one.

The group leader began, "We can talk about anything you want. Let's introduce ourselves and tell why we're here. It's as good a way as any to break the ice. Then we can talk." Afterwards she asked, "Who wants to begin?"

Perhaps to reassure herself, Joyce talked about the way she felt. "I just feel bored and empty. I don't know what's the matter with me. Maybe I should go to a doctor."

"All a doctor is going to do," Marie replied, "is give you some pills. Sure, the tranquilizers will make life easier for you. They'll dull your emotions so you can handle things. But they won't solve the problem, they won't help you face anything. Sure, you go to a doctor and have a check-up if you want. But don't use the pills to avoid your problems. That's stupid."

"Oh, I don't agree with you," Carol said. "I felt the same way, Joyce, for a long time. I finally went to a doctor, and I took tranquilizers for a while. I was terribly nervous, and they helped me pull myself together. They gave me a chance to get over a bad period. I mean, I think everybody gets bored and depressed once in a while, even if she has the most exciting job in the world, which—let's face it—being a housewife certainly isn't. It's just human to get depressed sometimes. And the repetition of the routine has to get you down occasionally. Anyhow, my mood passed after a few weeks.

"You know what helped me the most, I think. I hired a maid, who comes once a week. That way I have a day off. She's great. She does the heavy work, and I take off. I go shopping or to a movie or an art gallery or a play, if one's in town. It's my day for myself and it does me a world of good. My husband agrees with me, too. We laugh about my day off, about the fact that now I'm only a six-day housewife. But I rarely get depressed anymore because I have something to look forward to, some time of my own."

"I would," Elaine answered. "Even on a six-day week, I'd get depressed. I hate housework, I always did. And I'm pretty bad at it, too. Fortunately, we have a girl who comes in three days a week, and she does all the cleaning. I'd like to go to work, but with Beth, who's three, I don't feel right about looking for a job now. I'd just feel too guilty if I weren't home when Beth came back from nursery school. My mother worked when I was young, and I still remember that sinking feeling when I entered an empty house. I don't want my children to experience it. So I guess for a few years I'm pretty well trapped in the house, at least during the afternoons. But I make certain I go out a lot, particularly in the evenings. I do lots of volunteer work. And my husband is really terrific about baby-sitting. Right now, I'm involved with the League of Women Voters. It's great. I do something useful—helping people to register, informing them about the issues and the candidates. I feel that I'm doing something important, probably a lot more important than I would if I were working in an office just to make money."

"Well, the money is important to me," Rose said, "and I decided to work even though I have a child in the first grade. Oh, I guess I felt guilty at first. We didn't really need the money, although, of course, it comes in handy, and Jack's used to it now. But I felt that I had to work, had to make money, for my own self-respect. I believe that in our society you're judged on money. It's a way of saying whether or not what you do—and who you are—is worthwhile. At first, I tried working part-time, but it really took the whole day anyhow, by the time I got ready, went to work, and returned home. I still had to take care of the house, and I felt that I was working two jobs at the same time. Being employed full-time is easier for me. We hired a housekeeper. She's in the house until I get home from work, and she does all the cleaning, ironing, and shopping, as well as taking care of the kids. Now when I get home, all I do is cook dinner. I prefer things that way. I feel that I'm a more interesting person because I've got a life of my own. I enjoy being with my husband and children more than I did, too, because I don't feel so trapped. Also, I just like working. Meeting people, I don't feel isolated anymore. And my boss is great, really great. He's a tax lawyer, and he's training me to be his assistant. Of course, I'll probably never earn as much money as a man. Even when I become his assistant, I won't make much more than I am now. But it's worth it to me. Just being able to get out of the house is worth it to me. I feel stimulated and alive."

Sheila remarked, "Oh, maybe you will for a while, but working in an office gets boring, too, just like everything else. You know I divorced my husband a year ago. No particular reason. One day I was just looking at him and the house, and I thought, 'I've got to get away from here.'

"He's a nice guy, and we're still friends. We chat every Saturday when he visits the children. But I just couldn't continue living with him in that house. All those years of marriage, the boring daily routine of living with him, sat on me like a cloud. I felt I was suffocating. We'd talked so much, we knew each other so well, that we didn't have anything to say anymore. We had become two strangers who happened to share the same house. You know we're better friends now since the divorce. We lead separate lives and have lots to say to each other.

"But working is harder than I expected. I have a B.A. in English, and at first I thought I'd get a job teaching, but jobs are hard to find now, particularly for an older woman with no experience. I ended up in a typing pool, which wasn't what I wanted at all. Well, what can an English major do? Anyhow, it pays my expenses. My husband supports the children, of course, but I didn't ask for alimony. He doesn't make a lot of money, and I thought I should pay my own way, particularly since I was the one who wanted the divorce. But it's not easy, and money is really tight. I seem to be struggling to make ends meet. You know, I've even learned how to sew, something I swore I'd never do. It saves money, though.

"The worst thing for me is the loneliness. Everyone I know is married, they're our friends, and there is a strain now whenever I see them. At first they used to invite me to dinner often, but recently I haven't heard from them. I guess an extra woman can be troublesome, can make for an uncomfortable situation. I think they see my husband more often. It's different with a man. An extra man is useful and easier to handle socially, although, in general, married couples tend to invite other couples. It's just natural. I can't blame them. I used to do the same thing when I was married.

"But I have a hard life. I leave the children at the baby-sitter's and then go to work. I have to pick them up on my way home, make dinner for us all, do the laundry, clean, and play with them. By the time they're in bed, I'm ready for bed myself. I guess it would be easier if I had some friends. You know I'm more isolated now than I was before, when I was married. If I had known what it would be like, I wonder whether I would have divorced my husband. Of course, it's too late for us now, but I'd like to meet someone else. I'd really like to marry again, just for the companionship. But who wants to marry a thirty-four year old woman with two small children?"

"That's exactly why I didn't do what you did when I left my husband," Terry boomed. "We're in the process of getting a divorce now. I thought life might be too difficult. I remember exactly why I left—literally left—just walked out of the house, leaving a note.

"I'd been married nineteen years, and one day I was sitting in the kitchen, feeling depressed, feeling old, tired, and ugly, just as though whatever life I had promised myself had died long ago. It sounds funny, perhaps, but I felt like I didn't exist, as though I was a non-person, some robot who performed duties like cleaning the house, playing with the children, going out with my husband on Saturday nights. I felt as though I wore an identification tag, you know, the kind that says, "Hello, my name is. . . . ' But mine read, 'Hello, I'm Alice's mother' or 'Jay's wife.' The tag was like a key to a drawer of personalities. When I was 'Alice's mother' that's all I was, all I'd talk about. Nobody ever knew me because I was always somebody else. And I felt that I was sinking into my own nothingness, that if I didn't find out who I was, if I didn't wear my own tag, one that said, 'Hello, I'm *me*, I'm *Terry*,' I would die, just curl up and die.

"So I walked out, on the spur of the moment. I left Jay a note that said, 'Jay, I'm going. I have to have a life of my own. As soon as I find a room, I'll write. Please don't look for me. I'll be just fine. Give my love to the children, and tell them I'll miss them.'

"I took the housekeeping money, about thirty dollars, and a small overnight case. I left without any idea of where I was going. I moved here because it is only a few hours away from where we lived. I chose it because it was far enough away to give me a chance to live on my own and yet near enough to enable me to see the kids.

"I got a job right away. With thirty dollars, I had to. You know, I had never worked at all. I was married the summer I graduated from high school and Larry was born before our first anniversary. I was scared, I'll tell you. The day I applied at the department store, my hands were so damp I had to hold a hand-kerchief. But I was lucky. I got the job. The money isn't much, of course, but for me, alone, it's enough.

"That's one reason I left the kids with Jay. I knew I couldn't make it with them. It would be too much of a struggle. Also, I felt that it was better for them to stay with him. If I went alone, their lives were less disrupted. They would still be in the same house, the same neighborhood, with the same friends. If I'd taken them, they would have had to begin over again, too. And I didn't think that was right for them. Why should the mother have to get custody of the children?

"Maybe you think I'm selfish, but I thought if there is a divorce the man goes free. Oh sure, he misses the family and he supports the children, but he's free to begin again, to meet people, while the woman is trapped and burdened. She can't do what she wants. She still isn't her own person. She's just a mother without a husband. Well, maybe I am selfish, but I felt that I should have the same right as a man, the right to pick up my own life, to begin again.

"It's tough, but I'll never go back. I see the kids about twice a month, and we have a good time together. I'm like a sister now or a maiden aunt. Since I'm not bothering them all the time, I think we're better friends, particularly my daughter and I. She's twelve, the boys are nineteen, thirteen, and eight. I feel that I'm showing her that life doesn't have to be the way it was for me, that a woman doesn't have to follow the routine of marriage and housework and raising children.

"But I agree with Sheila. It's hard doing it alone, especially on my salary. I've met a couple of other women, one who did what I did, another who is divorced and has a twelve year old daughter. We're thinking of renting a house together, sort of a commune, where we share expenses and housework. If we do, I'd like to have my daughter come live with us.

"You know, we've been talking about helping others, maybe using the house as a way station for newly divorced women or women who have just been released from prison. We think we could really help them. The worst thing about breaking the mold is the loneliness. If we could group together and help each other, life would be easier for all of us. Of course, we're just talking now, trying to decide what to do and how to make it work. But I know we'll do something, and I'm certain it will be better than what I had or have now."

When the meeting was over, Joyce felt better. She knew she wasn't unique, that the women in her group had faced the same problem. She was excited, too, because the group had offered her so many solutions, solutions she had not even considered. But she was also frightened. She had to solve her own problem in her own way.

"What's right for me?" she asked herself. "What should I do?"

## Thelma: Living in Poverty

My name is Thelma Mays. I was born near Palm Beach, Florida, on May 29, 1948. I'm married, and I have two kids, Alvin, seven, and Dorie, four. I came to Washington, D.C., three years ago. I'm on welfare.

We were always poor. I don't know why, maybe because there were just too many of us. My father was a handyman. He tried to work steady but it was hard. Not enough jobs around, I guess. But my mother worked all the time. We needed the money so she did laundry. I remember her getting up early, going out everyday to pick it up, washing and ironing from dawn to dusk, even in the summer heat, and it sure gets hot around Palm Beach. She was always tired.

We lived in a kind of lean-to shack on a little land in Strawberry Bottom. I don't think we owned the land, but nobody ever bothered us. You know, my father built our house. It had four rooms, and goodness, we had beds all over that house. Me and my three sisters used to sleep on the floor. It was sure a small room. When the mattresses were down—we picked them up during the day to keep them from getting musty—you could hardly close the door. To get to the other side of the room, you'd have to step over the mattresses or edge yourself around the walls, being careful not to step on anybody. It was like a game. My six brothers slept in the other bedroom, on the floor, too. But they were really crowded together because there were more of them. I used to be glad I was a girl because we had more space. It made me feel freer, I guess. My folks slept by themselves in the living room. My father said he liked his privacy.

Things weren't too bad. Some people had smaller houses, maybe with only one bedroom, so we felt kind of rich. Of course, we all used outhouses, and we didn't have bathtubs or showers. But my father fixed up a cold water shower outside, and we used that when the weather was good. When it wasn't we just heated some water on the stove and washed in the kitchen sink.

It wasn't too bad, though, at least now when I look back on it. It was warm in Florida, not like here in D.C. There was lots of open country, too, and we could always play outside; we could always go off by ourselves if we wanted to. We never went hungry, either. My folks had a garden and we managed right well. Of course, we ate lots of grits, but we weren't starving.

But I didn't want to stay around home. All I could look forward to was being a waitress or a maid or marrying some poor guy like my father. I guess I was afraid I'd end up like my mother, worn out from too many kids and washing out other people's dirt.

I knew I'd never go to college or amount to anything. The school was bad. It wasn't teaching me much, and I'm not a good learner. I had okay grades, I guess, mostly "Cs," but I knew I couldn't do anything much with them. I'd need money to go to school, and nobody was going to give it to me. Even my folks knew that. Anyhow, if anybody was going to go to college, my dad wanted it to be my brother Harold. He was the oldest and really smart. But he quit school and joined the Army. He finished high school there, but then he went and joined up again and they sent him to Viet Nam. He was killed two years ago. What a waste! He was a good boy.

You know one of us did make it to college, after all, and it was my sister Marie. She was always real smart too, just like Harold, and she ended up getting herself some kind of small scholarship to Florida State.

The rest of us never are going to amount to anything much, although as far as I know I'm the only one who ever went on welfare. The rest are like my folks, I guess, just poor. We don't write much so I'm not too sure what's happening down there.

Maybe none of this would have happened to me if I hadn't quit school and married Josh. But I wasn't a good student and by the time I was sixteen, I wanted things. You know, pretty clothes, a little money of my own, a feeling of being somebody. The folks were mad about it, but I didn't see what difference it could make. I'd end up with the same kind of job; the education wasn't going to do me any good. So I quit as soon as I could, and I was really lucky. I got a waitress job in a small cafe where the tips were good. I was proud of myself.

I met Josh at the cafe. He was a migrant, but born in Florida, too. He'd followed the stream all his life. Of course he didn't have much schooling, and he couldn't write or read because migrant kids don't have much chance to go to school. They just don't stay anywhere long enough. But he was a beautiful man—eighteen, tall, husky, and big. I fell in love with him right away. He was just exciting to be with. I'd never been out of Florida, and here was a man who had traveled almost the whole country.

We got married a few months later. My folks weren't too happy about that, but what could they do? I was mad about him, and if we hadn't married, I would have run off with him anyhow.

We joined the stream. It was what Josh knew, and I wanted to travel, to get away from Palm Beach. I wanted to see the world and leave Florida forever, if I could. The stories we heard about life in the North! It seemed to me the streets were paved with gold, that diamonds must be sitting around waiting for me to pick them up,

Of course, working crops wasn't what I'd thought it would be. From a distance, there seemed to be so much money in it. I thought we'd be rich in just a couple of years, that if we wanted to we could buy us our own small farm.

We hitchhiked down state to work the orange groves. But jobs were harder to find than we'd figured. I couldn't work at all. The crew chief said he could get someone better for the same pay. Josh worked, though. He worked ten hours a day, climbing ladders and picking the fruit. He brought home about six dollars to eight dollars a day, which wasn't too bad. But we had to live in a company house, and they charged us fifteen dollars a week for that one-room shack. It was dirty, worse than anything I'd ever seen in my life. What I remember most about it was the mud— mud everywhere you went. You could smell the toilets, too. There was no water in the shack, not even a sink. I got the water from a leaky pipe, and I had to carry it back in a bucket and boil it before I could use it.

Of course, we were happy enough. We were young and just married. Josh kept telling me things would get better as we moved North, that I'd be able to work and we could save money. It was just a poor year in the groves, he said, because there'd been a freeze, and the crops weren't good.

We left after a couple of months. A crew chief for some peach farmers in Georgia came through and hired us. We paid him to take us up around Macon. It took all of our money just to get there. But we both worked—Josh on the ladders, me on the ground. It was sure hard work. I'd come home so tired I'd barely notice where I was. All I wanted to do was eat something quick and go to sleep. I used to keep a real clean house but after that job I got out of the habit. It just seemed too much trouble.

We moved North, working the crops, all the way to Jersey. Most of the time, we picked on the ground—lettuce, tomatoes, strawberries, cucumbers, stuff like that. I bent over so much that my back began to feel like a pretzel.

I got pregnant the first time in Jersey. I didn't even realize it. I thought I was tired from all that bending. I kept on working and, of course, I lost the baby. Josh felt real bad about it, but, I told him, "Don't worry. We'll have lots of kids." I lost three babies before Alvin came. I don't know why. Maybe working the crops and traveling so much did it. Yet, I worked when I was pregnant with Alvin. I had to, we needed the money. By the time we'd paid everyone off—the crew chief for hiring us or transporting us, the company for the shacks, the store for the food—we didn't have much left, I'll tell you. Sometimes, too, if crops were bad, there wasn't any work and no money. We went on welfare a couple of times, the longest being right after Alvin was born. I was sick, and Josh didn't want to leave, and there wasn't a job anywhere. Lord knows, he looked, but because he can't read and write, even though he's a hard worker, he just can't seem to find anything out of the stream. When I was better, we went back to the stream.

After a few years, though, I wanted to get out again, forever, even if we didn't have much money saved. I guess I got tired of bending and picking, reaching and picking, and coming back to a shack that was worse than a slum. And I had to take Alvin with me into the fields so that I could watch him. I kept thinking that's no way for my kid to grow up. I lost two more babies, too. When I got pregnant with Dorie, we decided that I should stop working, because Josh and I wanted another baby. I kept nagging him to leave the stream, so Josh promised we would before Dorie was born. Wherever we were, he said, we'd leave the stream, we'd go to the biggest city around, and he'd try to get a good job, steady work like loading trucks.

We ended up in Washington because John had been picking apples in the Shenandoah. We were really glad to be here at first. It was a large city but friendly. We found us a decent place to live, and Josh went out looking for work. For three months, with the debts growing so fast we could hardly remember what we owed, he looked. But he couldn't find anything because of his lack of schooling. He really tried, tried hard. He'd come back after looking, such a big powerful man, all curled up because he felt so small.

That's why he left me. He just couldn't stand it anymore, going out with hope and coming back defeated every day. We'd run out of money so bad that I wanted us to go on welfare right away. I guess he was ashamed, him being a grown man, a big, handsome man, a man who couldn't support his wife and kids. He loved us, you see. So he left, went back into the stream. Of course, he told me he was going and he promised to send money. He didn't, but I hadn't really thought he would. For the first six months, I heard from him once in a while. He'd get somebody to write out a card for him. But I haven't heard from him for a long time now. I hope he's all right. I don't blame him, you see. He tried, but there was nothing he could do. He didn't desert us, the way welfare people say. He just left us. So far I've been true to him. I care for Josh a lot.

I had to go on welfare the day he left. There was nothing in the house to eat. The social worker was nice. She got us emergency fund money until I could pick up a regular check.

We had to move, of course. The landlord didn't want welfare cases. He said they run down a property. So we're living here now in this slum, with the walls peeling from dampness and the water always brown from the rusty pipes. You know, once I caught a rat sitting on Dorie's bed. I was scared, and I went right down to that welfare office and complained. I really yelled. They're trying to find us a better place, maybe move us into the projects, but it's hard. Right now we're stuck here.

I don't know what to do. I really don't. I'm scared of living here. The place is awful. There are lots of robberies in this part of D.C., too, and sometimes I've seen addicts hiding in the hall. I don't want my kids growing up here.

I've thought about going back home, but I'm ashamed. And I guess things are bad there too. I left with such pride that I can't go home and tell the folks that Josh left me with the two kids.

I've thought of working, trying to get a waitress job again or even going out to do day work as a maid. There are lots of maid's jobs. The pay's not too good, though. And who would take care of the kids? Anyhow, if I do go back to work, the money I make comes off the welfare check. I figured it out. I'd make less by working than by just staying on welfare. And we don't do so well now because they took away the clothing allowance. We have to buy clothes out of the food money, which isn't so good because Alvin is a big eater. Anyhow I don't want to end up doing somebody's cleaning or washing.

But I'm getting restless and nasty staying in the apartment all the time. I feel blue. Sometimes I think I ought to just take the kids and go back to the stream. But I hate that life, and it's bad for the kids. They'd grow up to be migrants just like their father.

I wish I'd finished high school. Then maybe I could raise the kids right. The social worker said I should go to school at night. But who'd stay with the kids? Anyhow, I'm afraid to walk around here after dark. That's asking for trouble.

But this isn't a good life for the kids or me. I'm afraid of how they'll grow up, afraid they'll turn bad like that gang of boys who patrol the street, stealing groceries and money. I don't want them to be poor forever. I want them to have a good life, better than mine. And I don't want to stay on welfare. It makes me feel cheap, as if I'm no good myself.

I talked to the social worker about all this. She's a nice lady. She said maybe I ought to get rid of the kids, try to have them adopted or put them in foster homes, so that I could go back to school and learn a trade, become a typist or a lab technician or maybe even a practical nurse. She says it isn't fair to the kids to be brought up on welfare, with no man in the house. She says a lot of people would love to have Dorie because she's so young and pretty. Alvin might be a problem. He's kind of old for adoption. But she says I won't have any trouble finding a foster home. Of course, if I put them both in foster homes, I could always get them back, once I was working and making enough.

If I left the kids, I could look for Josh. Maybe he'd come back to me. If he learned to read and write, I know he'd be able to get a good job. If we were both working, we could make it easy, have a decent life for ourselves and the kids. I'd like that, I'd like Josh home with us. Maybe I should leave the kids for a while. But I don't know. I can't decide.

If I let someone adopt Dorie, I'd never see her again. It might be better for Dorie, but I don't know if I could do that. Who knows what the foster parents would be like? Would they love the kids? The social worker said she didn't think they'd be put in the same family. The kids wouldn't even live like family; they'd be apart. And suppose something happened to me? Or suppose I couldn't come back? At least now we're together.

But maybe being together isn't the right thing for the kids. Maybe I'm just being selfish because I want them with me.

Oh, I don't know what's right. I don't know what to do.

## Rita: Planning for the Future

Mrs. Selma Higgins is preparing a sociological study of the aspirations of high school students. During the week she spent at Somerset High, she talked with fifty students, all of whom had volunteered. Rita Stewart is one of the students she interviewed.

SELMA: Before we begin, could you tell me a little about yourself. Say anything you think would help me understand you.

RITA: Well, I really don't know what to say. I'm Rita Stewart, and I'm sixteen years old. I'm in the eleventh grade. I've lived in Somerset for the last ten years. We moved here from Salt Lake City when my father's company transferred him. My father is a corporation lawyer.

S: Do you have any brothers or sisters?

R: Yes. There's George, who's ten, and Sally, who's fourteen. George is in the fifth grade, Sally's in the ninth. She'll be coming over here next year.

S: Do you like them?

R: Well, you know how boys are. I mean, George can be a terrible nuisance. Sally's okay, though, just in that giggly stage. Oh, I guess I do, though, really. But it's hard to be the oldest. I feel responsible for them, and my mother is always expecting more of me because I am the oldest and a girl. George gets away with murder. When I was ten, I had to help around the house—set the table, dust, do the dishes. Sally did, too. But no one asks George to do anything. So he's spoiled, being the baby and a boy.

S: Does your mother work?

R: No. My Dad makes a very good salary, and Mom says she has too much to do around the house to go back to work now. Anyhow, I don't think Dad would like it. He believes a woman's first duty is to her husband and children. She does some volunteer work, though, with the church. Once a week, a group of them go to Harrington State, that's a hospital for the mentally retarded, and they act as nurses' aides, helping them feed the kids and playing with them.

S: How much education does your father have?

R: Well, he graduated from law school, at Stanford, that's in California.

S: And your mother?

R:    Mother went to Stanford, too. That's where they met. She didn't finish, though. They got married in her junior year. She quit to work so that Dad could finish. She worked as a secretary until he was through and could take over supporting her.

S:    How does she feel about it?

R:    I guess she wishes she had finished. At least, she is always telling me that I should go to college and get a degree so that I can get a good job. But I'm not sure she means it.

S:    I don't follow you.

R:    Well, she keeps telling me the best life for a woman is a good marriage, with a loving husband and kids. I don't see why you have to go to college just to become a wife and mother. Unless I go there just to get married—to meet somebody like Dad, you know, a man who's going to be a doctor or a lawyer, who'll make a good salary so you can be sure of having a decent life.

S:    Do you want to go to college?

R:    I'm not sure. I guess I do. At least everybody expects me to. I'm a good student, all "As" and "Bs," so I can go almost any place. It might be fun, I suppose. Anyhow, I don't think I want to go to work right after I graduate. I'd like to have fun for a while longer before I settle down into a routine. And I don't mind studying. I like to learn new things.

S:    Why do you sound so hesitant?

R:    Well, it sounds silly, I guess, but I'd like to take a year off after I graduate and do something different.

S:    Like what?

R:    Oh, I don't know—maybe just travel or work on a commune. A friend of mine is living on one now; she says it's great. I'd like to wander for a while, hitchhike around the country or maybe go to Europe and see all of it, not just as part of some fast tourist group, but on my own. You can do it cheaply, I know. A friend of mine, Paul, did it for three months. He said he lived on three dollars a day and it was great.

S:    Will you do it?

R:    I doubt it. I don't think my parents would approve. I mean, it's considered all right for a boy to do it, but not for a girl. Of course, it's easier for a boy, too. He can sleep almost anywhere, and it's safer for him to hitchhike alone. But I might do it, at least for a few months, if I could get courageous enough and could find somebody to go with me. But I don't know. The fights with the family hardly seem worth the trouble.

S: Why would you like to go?

R: To see things. You know I've led a sheltered life, like lots of people, I guess. This is a nice town, but most of it is the same. It's largely white, largely what you'd call middle-class. The poor live outside the town. I hardly ever see them, and it's almost as though they don't exist. We're all alike, my friends and I. We live in the same kind of houses, with nice yards, we eat the same kinds of things (you know, just plain American cooking), and we do the same kinds of things— movies, dances, sports, maybe sewing. I just don't think that's the way all of life is. I'd like to see how other people live, what it's like to be poor or to live in a different kind of society, where people make their living by fishing, for instance, or in Alaska. I guess it's not very clear. I've thought about it a lot, but it's hard to explain what I mean. It's just that I think life may be richer, more interesting, than it looks now. I'd like to know what's out there, so I could choose the way I want to live. I don't want to do the same old thing, to live the way my parents do.

S: What's wrong with the way they live?

R: Nothing really. It's a good life, and I've studied them; they look pretty happy with it. My Dad loves his job, he really does. I think maybe Mom isn't quite as happy. She's bored with housework. But she likes most of what she does most of the time. She has lots of friends and lots to do. But I'm not sure the way they live is right for me. The world is changing, I can feel it. Things are different now, and they'll be even more different when I'm as old as my parents. I mean nobody worried about the environment before or the atomic bomb or population. Nobody ever dreamed that we'd be walking on the moon. I keep feeling that I'm learning to live for the past, not for the future. And I don't know if that's the way to live. Of course, I don't know how else to live, either. Does anybody?

S: I doubt it. How would you like to live if you could?

R: Well, I guess I'd like to be comfortable. I'm spoiled, you know, used to living with space and in decent housing, with hot water, bathrooms, and heat. I've never been hungry or cold so I tend to take these things for granted. But I'd like them for everybody, not just for me, you know, for everybody in the United States and the rest of the world. Idealistic, I guess, but I'd like everybody to have enough. And I'd like to live in a world where I wasn't afraid. Most of us are, too afraid. We're afraid of war, of crime and the bomb and the dying land, the polluted water, the bad air. It's almost as though right now the world stands on the edge of death. I'm afraid for myself and for my kids.

S: Oh, you want children?

R: I think so. [Long pause] Yes, I know I do. Every woman wants children, doesn't she?

S: Probably most do. How many?

R: It's hard to say now. I think probably no more than two. I believe in controlling population, and I want to be able to do what's right for my kids.

S: Would you like to have a daughter?

R: Sure, even though I think life is harder for a girl.

S: Why?

R: Well, she's not as free, and she's tied to so many dull things, like cleaning house or going grocery shopping. And she can't learn anything she wants.

S: I don't understand.

R: Well, don't laugh, please. But you know we have to take a vocational course. Well, I like to read, and I just love books. To me, a beautiful book is a work of art. I wanted to take printing when I came to high school, so I went to the counsellor and told her. But she wouldn't let me. "Printing and woodworking are for boys; cooking and sewing are for girls." I argued with her, but I couldn't get permission, so I took sewing. It's good to know, I guess, but it's not what I wanted.

S: What did you want from high school that you feel you didn't get?

R: A few things, I guess. Except for printing, I could take anything I wanted. Don't laugh, but I like math and I love drafting. We did a little of it in one class, and I really enjoyed it. I like using my hands, too. And I like building things, putting odd pieces together. I'm good at it, too. I just have a knack for it, a sense of how to do it right. You know those confusing instructions on how to put something together, the ones that come with toys? My Dad can't do a thing with them. He's all thumbs, and it would be funny to watch him if he didn't get so mad about it. But I can do them, somehow I can figure them out and put the toy together fast. Now Dad usually tries once and if he can't do it, he asks me to do it for him. Of course, I pretend he's guiding me so he won't be too embarrassed. Actually, though, I'd get it done faster if he'd leave instead of watching me like some big boss. Neither of us says anything, though, but I think we both know I'm better with my hands than he is. [Long pause] To get back to your question, I'd like to have had courses in drafting, and more math, and maybe some courses in law or architecture.

S: Would you like to do work where you can use your hands?

R: Maybe. I took some tests, and it seems that I have an aptitude for it. The man who was testing me said, "You have an unusual ability to fit odd shapes together. You should be good at sewing." Sewing! Honestly, I was really angry. I don't even like to sew. And an aptitude like that should be good for something more serious than making my own clothes.

S: Like what?

R: Oh, maybe being an architect or an engineer.

S: Is that what you'd like to be, an architect?

R: No, I don't think so. If I had a choice, I'd rather be an engineer. I'm not too certain what they do besides build bridges. But I'd like something like that, figuring out how to build things, using math to plan. But I don't think I'll do it.

S: You could if you studied it in college.

R: I know, but if I went to college, I'm not sure I'd have the courage to major in engineering.

S: Why?

R: I'm just not sure they'd accept me. There don't seem to be many women engineers around.

S: Do you know any?

R: I met one once. She came to school to talk to a counselling class, to tell us what she did. It sounded interesting but a hard life for a woman. She had lots of trouble. She said she made almost straight "As" in her first two years in college. I think she said she made two "Bs" in English; she just wasn't any good at understanding literature. Anyhow, when she applied to the School of Engineering, she was turned down. The Dean told her that they really didn't think it was a profession for women. He urged her to do something more feminine, like teaching or nursing, or maybe, being a pediatrician. She was pretty discouraged. But her parents backed her, and she applied to a lot of other schools. She lost a year because she was trying to get into an engineering school.

Finally, she did. It wasn't a top one, though, not as good a school as she should have been in with her grades. She said it was hard. There was only one other woman in her class and about fifty men.

The teachers were all men, and they were harder on the women. She had to do better than the men to get the same grades. It wasn't obvious, of course, not so the teachers would get into trouble or she could complain. It was just a little harder, the answers had to be a little better. And some of the teachers weren't very nice. A couple of them were always making remarks like, "Here are the new breed of women," or "A pretty girl is a distraction." One professor (he must have been psychologically sick or something) used to make the two women sit apart, as though they carried a disease. Once he made them sit in front of the class for the whole period, while he quizzed them, making remarks to the rest of the class about how stupid they were. She said there wasn't anything they could do about the prejudice except quit. And by now she was determined to finish. So she swallowed it all—inside her. Just bottled up her anger in her. That can't be good for anybody.

When she talked to us, she sounded so bitter, so angry at men and the world that it hurt me. Nobody should be that angry; people shouldn't have to be filled with disgust and feel degraded. It has to change them.

Anyhow, she got a master's degree and decided to look for a job. Some of her teachers liked her, of course, one man in particular who, she said, was well known. He promised to help her. "But it will be a problem," he told her. "Most employers feel women, even smart women like you, aren't good bets. They feel that after they've spent money training you, you'll just get married, have children, and quit, that it's a waste of money to hire you." She asked him, "What do you want me to do, to write with my own blood a statement that I'll never marry or become pregnant?"

It took a long time for her to find work, but she did in a firm where the president was a friend of her teacher's. But she hasn't gone far. She said that men who started after her had better jobs and made almost twice as much as she did, even though her work was as good. She doesn't have a position of authority, either. Although she does the same work as the man in the next office, she's called an assistant. But she said that she was one of the first, she's been an engineer for twenty years, and that times may be changing. She believes if more women went into engineering (she said that now only about 1 percent of engineers are women, which is nothing practically), firms would come to look at them more objectively, would begin to give them equal jobs and salaries.

S: How many children does she have?

R: I forgot to tell you. She never married. I'm not sure why she didn't. We asked her, but all she would say was that she liked her freedom, that she didn't want to be tied down with a family. She may be sorry, though. Her life sounded very lonely. I felt that she'd made a choice between love and a career. And that's not right. I mean, why should somebody feel that she had to give up love just to do what she wanted? I guess she has problems of her own.

S: Do you want to get married?

R: Well, not right away, of course. But I guess so, someday. Being a girl, you naturally grow up expecting to get married and have children. And I'd like to love somebody, to have him love me. It's a good feeling, and I think love may be the most important thing in the world. I'd imagine that being without love must be hard, not having anybody to care for you, to care about you. I'd give up a lot to have that kind of love.

S: What do you mean?

R: Well, I'm not sure I'd be so serious about a career of my own if I were married. I guess in some ways I'm still pretty traditional. I'd hate to hurt somebody I love, to stop him from doing what he wants because of me. I keep thinking that a man's job ought to be more important, that he ought to come first.

S: But you don't sound very enthusiastic about it.

R: I have mixed feelings, I guess. The choice is too hard. I keep wondering why I have to make a choice like that. It's like choosing between what I want and the person I love wants. It's not a fair choice. We should both be able to do what we want.

S: Maybe you can. People are different. Let's get back to engineering for a minute. Do you think that if you go to college, you'll major in it?

R: I just don't know. I'd kind of like to try if I can. But I'm worried about it. Suppose things aren't different now? Suppose I have the same problems that woman who spoke to us did. My parents won't back me. In fact, I know my Dad wants me to be an English teacher. At least, he keeps telling me that's a good job for a woman because she can always go back to it after her children are older. Also, I don't want to become like that woman. I keep seeing her, filled with anger and disgust. I want more out of life than she has. And her life is hard. I mean she's good but she doesn't have the prestige a man does, not even the money. She sacrificed an awful lot.

I guess I'm afraid, too, afraid of competing with men. I like them, and I want to be loved. Suppose men don't like women who are serious about a career? I want to enjoy life. I don't want to devote myself to engineering 24 hours a day.

And there's another problem. I'm not sure that college is worth it, that having a career is worth it. What will the world be like in 20 or 30 years? Will engineers be needed? Suppose there is a world war or pollution gets out of control? Perhaps it would be better for me to live now, to grab all the happiness I can before everything dies. Nothing seems certain anymore, and I just don't know what I should do, or how, or with whom. I thought maybe you'd help me see things clearly, help me know what's right, help me make up my mind. What do you think?

S:  I don't know.

R:  What should I do? Please tell me, what should I do?

## An Overview of Women in American History

In her fascinating book, *The First Sex*, Elizabeth Gould Davis presents a history of women's contributions to civilization since the first millenium. She contends, from her study of history, archaeology, mythology, and science, that women's contributions have been superior to men's and that man is actually a biological mutant, while women are the "first sex." Robert Graves, in *The Greek Myths*, notes that in prehistoric times man was dominated by woman and was considered weaker, less worthy, and even despised. Davis indicates that men became resentful of women's superiority and, through physical strength, conducted an ancient patriarchal revolution that replaced the idea of female natural dominance with male natural dominance. This, Davis argues, explains the long history of sexual inequality that has kept women subservient to men.

While one may question whether Elizabeth Gould Davis is right or not, it is clear throughout recorded history that women have had to fight for equal treatment. Consider these examples.

*In Colonial America*

Girls were admitted to school only during summer session, while the boys harvested. "Girls should not be meddling in such things as are proper for the men whose minds are stronger," said John Winthrop, governor of the Massachusetts Bay Colony.

Women could expect to die before their husbands because of hard work and inadequate medical care in childbirth. The husband was the sole guardian over children. He had complete control over his wife's actions. Divorces were seldom granted. Many women ran away from their husbands. Women were generally thought of as inferior *but* consider:

*Anne Hutchinson*: Widely known for her skills in midwifery and healing with herbs, she preached religious freedom and individual conscience. Found guilty of heresy, she was banished from the Massachusetts Bay Colony. After moving to Rhode Island and then to Long Island, she and most of her family were killed by Indians in 1643. She was the first American woman to preach to women.

*Margaret Brent*: One of two sisters who owned large estates in Maryland, she was a legal spokesman for other women and earned the distinction of serving as executor of Governor Calvert's will. In 1647 she became the first American woman to seek the vote and political office. She was permitted to vote as the Governor's attorney, but was not seated in the Maryland Assembly.

## After the Revolution, in the New Nation

Increased opportunity for the education of certain women led to cultured, elite ladies for the upper classes. Since "woman's place is in the home," women were educated to be housewives, mothers, and charming companions to their husbands.

Professions became restrictive in licensing practitioners and women were excluded. A shortage of men for teaching jobs in New England provided opportunities for large numbers of women to become teachers. But most jobs for women resulted from industrialization and were for low wages and long hours in factories.

Although the first woman's mass circulation magazine, *All Lady Repository*, was produced in 1792, the idea of women writers was not popularly accepted until the 1830s. Nathaniel Hawthorne described them as "that mob of scribbling women."

Yale examined twelve year old Lucinda Foote in 1783 and determined her to be "fully qualified, except in her sex, to be received as a pupil of the freshman class of Yale University."

"A very little wit is valued in a woman, as we are pleased with the few words of a parrot," Jonathan Swift said in an appraisal of English women.

Feminist ideas began to develop in response to the degradation of women during the colonial period. The English writer Mary Wollstonecraft published *A Vindication of the Rights of Women* in 1791 in which she protested the domination of women's minds by men, and the book received a great deal of attention in America.

## In the Nineteenth Century

Education for the professions of law and medicine was denied to women until mid-century. After the Civil War, some colleges began to open to women.

Nursing and teaching were the primary jobs for educated women, and these fields offered low pay and held a low social status.

Factory work and home labor on piecework were the main employment for women. Both were for long hours and low salaries. Women typically held the most unskilled and lowest status jobs.

Women in the West fared much the same as women had in the colonial period, while in the southern states white women were idolized for their feminine charm but not for their minds, and black women were seen only as workers and slave breeders.

The earliest movement for reform in social welfare began to develop from church groups and sewing circles. Reformers included the Grimké sisters and Lucretia Mott, who were strong anti-slavery advocates; Dorothea Dix who campaigned for improvements in prisons and other institutions; and Elizabeth Cady Stanton, a leader in women's rights.

The first convention on women's rights, which took place in 1848 at Seneca Falls, New York, held that women were the equal of men, but only Charlotte Woodward of the 260 women present lived long enough to see women get the vote in America.

Sarah Grimké and Margaret Fuller wrote strong books arguing for the equality of women. Susan B. Anthony became a leader in the women's suffrage movement.

## In the Early Twentieth Century

Many schools still had separate entrances for girls and boys.

The National Women's Trade Union League was formed during the 1903 AFL Convention to organize women workers.

Sweatshop labor—long hours and low pay—was performed by women and children, but new laws provided some protections from fire, excessive work hours, and heavy loads.

World War I led to many more women in skilled industrial jobs, but the depression made the job market male dominated again. World War II opened jobs to women.

Maria McCleod Bethune, who started schools for girls, became the first black woman to head a federal agency.

The National American Woman Suffrage Association was formed in 1890 to heal splits among the major women's suffrage groups. After years of protests, demonstrations, writings, meetings, and very limited successes, the Nineteenth Amendment to the U.S. Constitution was ratified in 1920, and women were able to vote.

*Contemporary America*

The very brief overview just presented suggests a long tradition of sexual inequality. The rest of this book is devoted to an understanding of the status of women in contemporary America.

# Chapter 2

# Women's Educational

# and Employment Status

This chapter contains information to assist in understanding the educational and employment status of women in the United States today. Remember, however, that America is changing rapidly and that, in particular, the status of women is changing. What changes seem to be occurring?

### What Is a Woman?

The most obvious place to look for a definition is in the dictionary. According to the unabridged *Webster's New International Dictionary*, a woman is:

1. An adult female person, as distinguished from a man or child; sometimes, any female person, often as distinguished from *lady*.
   *Women* are soft, mild, pitiful, and flexible. *Shak.*
2. The typical member of the female sex; — used as a generic singular without an article; the female part of the human race; womankind.
   Man is destined to be prey to *woman. Thackeray.*
3. With *the*. Distinctively feminine nature, qualities, characteristics, or disposition; womanhood; womanliness; as, subduing the *woman* in her; — sometimes in the phrase *the woman of it*, the characteristically feminine factor, action, response, reaction, or the like.
4. A female attendant or servant.
5. a A paramour; mistress. b pl. Females as partners in sexual intercourse or irregularities; as, to refrain from *women.*

6. A wife. *Familiar*.

7. A female person of a position, calling, or standing, specified in a phrase with *of*; as, a *woman* of breeding, of color, of title; a *woman* of all work, of letters; the *woman* of the house; often in contemptuous epithets connoting easy virtue; as, a *woman* of pleasure, of the town, of the streets.

8. The reverse of a coin, originally as bearing figure of Britannia. *Brit*.

9. Bringer of woe; — by whimsical etymological derivation from *woe + man*. *Obs*.

A fuller understanding of the significance of the definition occurs when derived words are also defined.

Womanish: 1. Of or belonging to a woman or women; done or worn by women. *Now Rare*. 2. Resembling or suitable to a woman; having the qualities of a woman; woman-like; effeminate; not becoming a man; — usually disparaging.
Thy tears are *womanish. Shak*.

Womanly: 1. Possessed of the qualities peculiar to or characteristic of women, esp. the qualities proper or becoming to women, as gentleness, compassion, modesty; befitting or characteristic of a woman; woman-like; feminine; effeminate; as, *womanly* behavior. "*Womanliest* tenderness" *Zangwill*. 2. Possessed of the character or behavior befitting a grown woman; no longer childish or girlish; becoming to a grown woman. 3. Belonging to or done by female persons. 4. Actuated by or conforming to woman's nature.

## What Is a Man?

As you compare these terms defining woman with those defining man, ask yourself how the definitions reflect different attitudes about the sexes.

Man: I. A member of the human race.

1. A human being; a person; — now restricted to males except in general applications; as, every *man*; few *men*.
All *men*, both male and female. *Hume*.

2. The human race; mankind; human beings collectively
And God said, Let us make *man* in our image. *Gen*.i.26.

3. a human form and nature as a mode of being; as, God became *man*. b The material or spiritual parts of a human being; as, the inward *man*.

4. Individual; as: a Used in place of a pronoun, usually with sympathy; as, the good *man* fell ill. b Used for a present or former holder of office, esp. in depreciation; as, the late *man* (i.e., king). c Used in phrases, as in man by man, man to man. d The individual one requires or has in mind; — used after possessives; as, he's your *man*.

Our sailors had every one seized his *man*. *Marryat.*

5. With *a*, one, or anyone, indefinitely; — a modified survival of the Anglo-Saxon *man*, or *mon*, as an indefinite pronoun. "A *man* cannot make him laugh." *Shak.*

6. A supernatural being or creature. *Obs.*

No *man* means evil but the devil. *Shak.*

7. Manly character or quality; manhood; manliness.

It hath cow'd my better part of *man*. *Shak.*

**II**. A male human being.

8. The male human being; also, a human being or a male human being, as such, without regard to his accidents of position, office, etc.; esp., an adult male person.

The king is but a *man*, as I am. *Shak.*

9. a An adult male belonging to a (specified) classification, as by birth, residence, or membership; as, a college *man*; a medical *man*. Cf. —man. b A member of a military, naval, or similar force; as, heavy losses in *men*. c Eng. An undergraduate.

10. a A married man; a husband; — correlative to *wife*. *Now Chiefly Dial.*, except in phr. *man and wife*. b A lover or suitor.

11. An adult male servant, as a valet; also, an adult male employee; — correlative of *master*; as, the *men* are on a strike. "Like master, like *man*." *Old Proverb.*

12. A term of familiar address often implying authority, impatience, or contempt; as, Come, *man*, we must go; my good *man*, what are you doing?

13. One possessing in a high degree the distinctive qualities of manhood; one having manly excellence.

Nature might stand up
And say to all the world "This was a *man*!" *Shak.*

14. A person of consequence or position; as, to make one a *man* forever; — often in the phrase of a *man or a mouse*.

15. A conical heap of stones set up on a mountain top; the mountain top itself; as, Scafell *Man. Local. Eng.*
16. The obverse of a coin; — so called in tossing. *Eng.*
Mannish: 1. Human. *Obs.* 2. Resembling, suitable to, or characteristic of, a man, as distinguished from a woman or from a child; manlike. Syn. — See MALE. Ant. — Feminine, womanly. See FEMALE.
Manly: 1. Human. *Obs.* 2. Having qualities becoming to a man; manlike; esp., brave; resolute; noble. Adult; mature. *Obs.* Syn. — Bold, daring, undaunted, hardy. See MALE. Ant. — Childish; womanish, effeminate; cowardly.

These definitions reflect cultural attitudes about men and women and suggest how they should behave. Let us look now at the ways women are trained for their sexual roles.

### Education for Sexual Roles

To a large extent all of us are taught what our role should be and what is right for us to do. This training begins as soon as we are born so that much of what we will become is decided before we are six. Consider these examples.

In Sunday School children learn about the creation of man. Indirectly, at the same time, they learn about woman's place and her role. As the *Bible* teaches us in the Book of Genesis:

21  And the Lord God caused a deep sleep to fall upon Adam, and he slept; and he took one of his ribs, and closed up the flesh instead thereof;
22  And the rib, which the Lord God had taken from man, made he a woman, and brought her unto the man.
23  And Adam said, This *is* now bone of my bones, and flesh of my flesh: she will be called Woman, because she was taken out of Man.
24  Therefore shall a man leave his father and his mother, and shall cleave unto his wife: and they shall be one flesh.

Children learn, too, that "the fall" of man is woman's fault. Beguiled by the serpent, Eve ate the forbidden fruit and gave it to Adam. As a result, Adam and Eve had to leave the Garden of Eden. Misery, sorrow, and mortality then came to mankind — all because of the first woman.

Parents frequently read nursery rhymes to their children. These also teach girls about their roles. As you read the well-known poems given below, ask yourself what qualities about a woman are considered to be the most important.

### Natural History

What are little boys made of, made of?
What are little boys made of?
　　Frogs and snails
　　And puppy-dog's tails,
That's what little boys are made of.

What are little girls made of, made of?
What are little girls made of?
　　Sugar and spice
　　And all things nice,
That's what little girls are made of.

What are young men made of, made of?
What are young men made of?
　　Sighs and ieers
　　And crocodile tears,
That's what young men are made of.

What are young women made of, made of?
What are young women made of?
　　Ribbons and laces
　　And sweet pretty faces,
That's what young women are made of.

### Proposals

　　Curly locks, Curly locks,
　　Wilt thou be mine?
　　Thou shalt not wash dishes
　　Nor yet feed the swine;
　　But sit on a cushion
　　And sew a fine seam,
　　And feed upon strawberries,
　　Sugar and cream.

*My Little Wife*

I had a little wife,
The prettiest ever seen;
She washed up the dishes,
And kept the house clean.
She went to the mill
To fetch me some flour,
And always got home
In less than an hour.
She baked me my bread,
She brewed me my ale,
She sat by the fire
And told many a fine tale.

Toys, particularly toys for young children, are an excellent indication of the roles expected of men and women. Following is a list of common toys. On a separate sheet of paper, make up three lists, one for boys, one for girls, and one for both. Place the toys into appropriate categories. After you have finished, ask yourself why you divided the toys as you did and what these divisions tell you about sexual roles.

> jump rope, gun, puzzle, blocks, model airplane, truck, embroidery kit, automobile, kite, broom, tea set, football, baseball bat, cards, doll, sewing machine, finger paints, ball, trumpet, piano, telephone, record player, pull toy.

In public schools, as children learn reading, writing, and arithmetic, they continue to learn about their sexual roles as well. A study of elementary school readers, prepared by Elisabeth Hagan and the Central New Jersey Chapter of the National Organization for Women, printed in the *Report on Sex Bias in the Public Schools* by the New York Chapter of NOW, showed:

> In a total of 144 readers examined (from fifteen reading series and ranging from primer to sixth grade level), there are 881 "amusing and exciting" stories centering around boys to 344 stories centering around girls. This represents 72% boy-oriented stories to cater to 49% of small boys in the elementary school population.
> Similarly, there are 282 stories centering around adult males to 127 stories centering around adult females. There

are 131 biographies of famous men to 23 biographies of famous women.

In the early grade readers the oldest child in a family is always a boy. Boys are associated with making, earning, playing active games, learning, romping with dogs and helping their fathers.

Girls are associated with helping their mothers or brothers, playing with kittens, getting into minor forms of trouble and being helped out by their brothers. Patterns of dependence, passivity and domesticity are apparent.

Two mathematics books examined reflected similar attitudes toward women's social roles. In *Seeing through Arithmetic Five* (Scott Foresman):

Page   45—Out of ten problems, five dealt with girls cooking and sewing.
Page   65—Problems dealing with club activities: girls are shown making sandwiches, while boys build dividers.
*Math Book 5* (Heath):
Page 155—Out of ten problems, five deal with boys working at physical activities, and two problems have girls babysitting and sewing.
Page 173—There are 12 problems altogether, eleven dealing with boys earning money, building things and going places, while one deals with a girl buying a ribbon for a sewing project.

In the case of Bonnie Sanchez and Laura Edelhart against Harold Baron, Principal of Junior High School 217, and Hugh McDougall, District Superintendent of District 28 of New York City, a law suit brought by the mothers of two female students because of sexual discrimination, the testimony indicates that girls are sometimes treated differently than boys in their curriculum and sports. Laura Edelhart, for example, was told that her daughter could not take metal work or mechanics because " . . . we have too many boys in the school to be able to allow the girls to take . . . " them.

Gigi Gordon, a ninth grade student, reported that girls were permitted to take sewing and cooking, while boys could take metal, printing, and ceramics.

Julie Nives, also a ninth grade student, testified that in gym:

"The boys do exercises. They play basketball. They can go out when it is warm, which the girls are not allowed to do. They play handball. Baseball. They have certain teams after school for just baseball, basketball, track teams, which the girls do not have. . . . We asked for basketball. They said there wasn't enough equipment. The boys prefer to have it first. Then we will have what is left over."

As these examples illustrate, the education of women can be affected by the attitudes about woman's role which make up part of our cultural heritage. Yet, according to the 1969 *Handbook on Women Workers*, published by the Women's Bureau of the Department of Labor, "The continuing growth of our economy depends in large measure on the amount of trained manpower or womanpower available."

The potential significance of woman's contribution to the economy of the United States becomes clear when we realize that women comprise more than 51 percent of the population. According to figures collected by the Census Bureau in 1970, there are 100 women for every 94.8 men. In addition, women live longer. The Department of Health, Education, and Welfare reports that as of 1968 (the latest figures available at the time of writing), the average life expectancy for white men was 67.5 years, but for white women it was 74.9 years; for nonwhite men, the average life expectancy was 60.1 years, while for nonwhite women it was 67.5.

## Education of Women

Since women are necessary to the economic well-being of the United States, the first question we should ask is, "Are they educated adequately?" There is no doubt that women are better educated than they have been in the past. For example, according to the Women's Bureau and the Department of Health, Education, and Welfare (Table 1), the number of women graduating from high school and college has increased greatly from 1900 to 1970.

It is worth noting, however, that as Table 2 indicates, the percentage of degrees earned by women is significantly less than the percentage earned by men. In addition, although the number of women receiving advanced degrees has increased, the percentage since 1930 has increased only slightly at the bachelor's level,

Table 1. Number of Women Graduates

|  | 1900 | 1970 |
| --- | --- | --- |
| High school graduates | 56,800 | 1,467,000 |
| Bachelor's or first | | |
| professional degrees | 5,200 | 346,373 |
| Master's degrees | 300 | 83,241 |
| Doctor's degrees | 23 | 29,872 |

*Sources:* Women's Bureau, Fact Sheet on Trends in Educational Attainment of Women, August, 1969, and Department of Health, Education, and Welfare, Earned Degrees Conferred, 1971.

Table 2. Percentage of College Degrees Earned by Women

| Year | Bachelor's degrees | Master's degrees | Doctor's degrees |
| --- | --- | --- | --- |
| 1900 | 19 | 19 | 6 |
| 1930 | 40 | 40 | 15 |
| 1969–70 | 42 | 40 | 13 |

*Sources:* Women's Bureau, Fact Sheet on Trends in Educational Attainment of Women, August 1969, and Department of Health, Education, and Welfare, Earned Degrees Conferred, 1971.

remained the same at the master's level, and actually declined at the doctoral level.

The percentage of women who receive college degrees, therefore, is not proportionate to the percentage of women in the general population. Why do you think this discrepancy exists?

The majority of women who receive college degrees tend, furthermore, to major in a limited number of fields. For example, according to figures given by the Department of Health, Education and Welfare, the largest number of bachelor and first professional degrees conferred on women during 1969–70 were in the fields shown in Table 3 on the next page.

Subjects men studied were pursued by few women. Compare the numbers of men and women who majored in the fields shown in Table 4 in 1969–70.

At the master's level, more than half of the degrees conferred on women in 1969–70 were in education (44,145 out of a total of 83,241). Next in popularity were degrees in social science, although the number decreases sharply (8,381). English and

Table 3.  Number of Degrees Earned by Women in Selected Fields for
1969–1970

| Field | No. of degrees conferred |
| --- | --- |
| Education | 124,819 |
| Social sciences | 57,886 |
| English and journalism | 40,259 |
| Fine and applied arts | 20,584 |
| Health professions | 17,954 |
| Foreign languages and literatures | 15,884 |
| Psychology | 14,741 |
| Nursing | 11,120 |
| Biological sciences | 10,514 |
| Mathematical sciences | 10,317 |
| | |
| Total conferred | 324,078 |

*Source:* Department of Health, Education, and Welfare, Earned Degrees Conferred, 1971.

Table 4.  Selected Fields of Study by Sex for 1969–70

| Field | Men | Women |
| --- | --- | --- |
| Architecture | 3,698 | 204 |
| Accounting | 96,760 | 9,519 |
| Dentistry | 3,712 | 36 |
| Law | 14,837 | 878 |
| Geology | 2,011 | 244 |
| Religion | 9,102 | 1,855 |

*Source:* Department of Health, Education, and Welfare, Earned Degrees Conferred, 1971.

journalism comprised the third most popular major (5,477). These were, of course, the three fields which most women undergraduates majored in.

On the doctoral level, education continued to be the most popular single degree for women (1,196 out of a total of 3,980). Social sciences remained the second choice (490). The third most popular field, however, shifted from English and journalism to biological sciences, in which 469 women received degrees.

This information about the education of women raises the following questions:

• Why do women tend to major in so few fields?
• Why do they choose the fields they do?

- How is the choice of these fields affected by the concept of woman's role?
- What is the relationship between women's education and women's work?

Let us turn now to the jobs women hold.

## Women and Their Work

*The Housewife*

Few people think of the housewife as a worker. A husband will say of his wife, "She's not working." A boy will say of his mother, "She just stays home all the time." Even the housewife herself is likely to tell someone, "Oh, I don't work. I'm just a housewife." The housewife doesn't draw a salary, and the value of her work is not recorded in the figures that make up the Gross National Product of the United States.

Yet according to an informal survey prepared by economists at Chase Manhattan Bank (Table 5), the average full-time housewife works a total of 99.6 hours a week, or an average of more than 14 hours a day, 7 days a week. She performs a minimum of 12 different jobs. If she were paid for these jobs at the 1972 hourly rates, she would receive a weekly salary of $257.53.

Table 5. A Housewife's Jobs

| Job | Hours per week | Rate per hour | Value per week |
|-----|----------------|---------------|----------------|
| Nursemaid | 44.5 | $2.00 | $89.00 |
| Housekeeper | 17.5 | 3.25 | 56.88 |
| Cook | 13.1 | 3.25 | 42.58 |
| Dishwasher | 6.2 | 2.00 | 12.40 |
| Laundress | 5.9 | 2.50 | 14.75 |
| Food buyer | 3.3 | 3.50 | 11.55 |
| Gardener | 2.3 | 3.00 | 6.90 |
| Chauffeur | 2.0 | 3.25 | 6.50 |
| Maintenance man | 1.7 | 3.00 | 5.10 |
| Seamstress | 1.3 | 3.25 | 4.22 |
| Dietitian | 1.2 | 4.50 | 5.40 |
| Practical nurse | .6 | 3.75 | 2.25 |
| Total | | | $257.53 |

*Source:* Chase Manhattan Bank.

The housewife, however, receives only what money her husband chooses to give her. In addition, her work is excluded from Social Security. As Ann Crittenden Scott pointed out in the July 1972 issue of *MS.* magazine, if a housewife

> . . . is widowed and at least 62, she receives only 82½ percent of the benefits he [her husband] had earned. If she is divorced, she receives nothing unless she was married at least 20 years and can show that he is contributing or was ordered to contribute to her support. And if she has worked outside the home for a time, as most women do, she must choose, upon retirement, either her own benefit or half of her husband's, whichever is larger. She can't receive both, even though both have been earned.

For these reasons, many consider the housewife to be a worker who is underpaid, overworked, and assured of little, if any, financial security. Do you agree?

## Women in the Labor Force

In addition to being housewives, a large number of married women hold full- or part-time jobs. In general, almost two out of every five workers are women. Of those women who work, three-fifths are married, one-fifth are single, and one-fifth are widowed, divorced or separated from their husbands.*

The myth that "women aren't seriously attached to the labor force, they work only for 'pin money'," can be easily dismissed. The Women's Bureau reports:

> Of the 32 million women in the labor force in March 1971, nearly half were working because of pressing economic need. They were either single, widowed, divorced, or separated or had husbands whose incomes were less than $3,000 a year. Another 5.4 million had husbands with incomes between $3,000 and $7,000 — incomes which, by and large, did not meet the criteria established by the Bureau of Labor Statistics for even a low standard of living for an urban family of four.†

---

* "Women Workers Today," 1971 (rev.), Women's Bureau, Department of Labor.
† "The Myth and the Reality," 1972, Women's Bureau, Department of Labor.

In "Women Workers Today" (1971), the Women's Bureau describes the employment characteristics of women workers as follows:

*Worklife patterns.*—Typically a woman enters the labor force after she has finished her schooling, works for a few years, and then leaves the labor force when she marries or has her first child. After her children are in school or are grown, she either goes back to paid employment or undertakes some type of community service. The return of mature women to the labor force has been a vital factor in the tremendous increase in the number of women workers in recent years — in 1970 half of all women 35 to 64 years of age were in the labor force, as compared with 1 out of 4 in 1940.

Currently 43 percent of all women 16 years of age and over in the population are workers. Of the 41 million women not in the labor force in 1970, 33 million were keeping house, 3½ million were students, and 2 million were out of the labor force because of ill health or disability.

*Full-time and full-year workers.* — About 7 out of 10 women workers have full-time jobs at some time during the year, but only about 4 out of 10 work at full-time jobs the year round. Girls 16 to 19 years of age, most of whom are in school, are least likely to be employed full time the year round — only 8 percent of those who worked at any time in 1969 were so employed. Women 45 to 64 years of age are most likely to be fully employed the year round (54 percent in 1969).

*Part-time workers.* — Part-time employment frequently is preferred by married women with family responsibilities (especially women with young children), students, and women 65 years of age and over. During recent years the shortage of skilled workers in many occupations has provided more opportunities for part-time as well as full-time workers. Thus, 11.7 million women worked at part-time jobs at some time during 1969. Part-time work is most common among farm, private household, and sales workers. But many women also hold part-time jobs as waitresses or cooks; stenographers, typists, or secretaries; teachers; and medical or other health workers.

The work women do is apt to be very different from that of men, as shown in Figure 1.

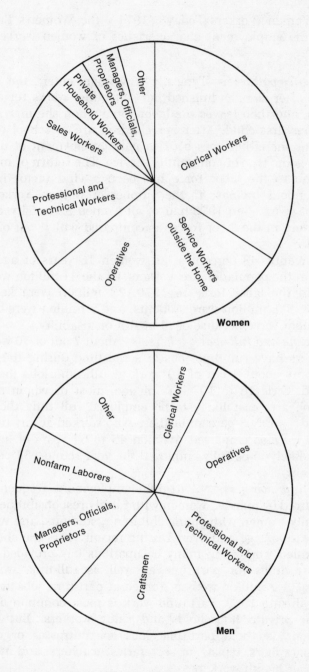

**Figure 1.** Occupations of employed workers in 1970, showing the occupational distribution of women compared with that of men. *Source:* Women's Bureau, "Women Workers Today," 1971 (rev.)

Women are more apt than men to be white-collar workers, but the jobs they hold are usually less skilled and less well paid than those of men. Women professional workers are most likely to be teachers, nurses, and other health workers, while men are most frequently employed in professions other than teaching and health. Women are less likely than men to be managers and officials, and are far more likely to be clerical workers.

Only 1 out of 6 women workers is employed in a blue-collar job, but almost half the men are in such jobs. Women are almost as likely as men to be factory workers, but are very seldom employed as skilled craftsmen — the occupation group for 1 out of 5 men workers.

More than 1 out of 5 women but only 1 out of 14 men workers is a service worker. Three-fourths of the women and virtually all of the men service workers are employed in occupations other than private household work.

In addition, as the Women's Bureau reports, "Unemployment rates are consistently higher for women than for men. . . ." For example, in 1970, 4.4 percent of men workers and 5.9 percent of women workers were unemployed. Moreover,

Women's annual earnings are substantially lower than those of men. Much of the difference is accounted for by the fact that women are more likely than men to have only part-time and/or part-year jobs. But even among workers fully employed the year round, women's median earnings are only three-fifths of those of men. . . .

According to the Bureau, the earnings gap between men and women was actually greater in 1970 ". . . than it was 15 years ago. From 64 percent in 1955, women's median wage or salary income as a proportion of men's fell to 61 percent by 1959 and 1960 and since then has fluctuated between 58 and 60 percent. Women's median earnings of $5,323 in 1970 were 59 percent of the $8,966 received by men." The Bureau reports:

The gap in earnings varies by major occupation group. It was largest in 1970 for sales workers (women earned only 43 percent of what men earned) and smallest for professional and technical workers (women earned 67 percent of what men earned). Wage or salary incomes of women in relationship to those of men were somewhat higher in 1970 than in 1969 for managerial workers, sales workers, and professional workers, but lower for service workers outside the home.

Although "The educational background of a worker often determines not only the type of work but also the level of job within an occupation for which he or she can qualify," the gap in earnings cannot be explained by differences in education, as Table 6 demonstrates.

Table 6. Median Income in 1970 of Full-Time Year-Round Workers, by Sex and Years of School Completed (Persons 25 years of age and over)

| Years of school completed | Median income | | Women's median income as percentage of men's |
|---|---|---|---|
| | Women | Men | |
| Elementary school: | | | |
| Less than 8 years | $3,798 | $6,043 | 62.8 |
| 8 years | 4,181 | 7,535 | 55.5 |
| High school: | | | |
| 1–3 years | 4,655 | 8,514 | 54.7 |
| 4 years | 5,580 | 9,567 | 58.3 |
| College: | | | |
| 1–3 years | 6,604 | 11,183 | 59.1 |
| 4 years | 8,156 | 13,264 | 61.5 |
| 5 years or more | 9,581 | 14,747 | 65.0 |

*Source:* Women's Bureau, Fact Sheet on the Earnings Gap, December 1971 (rev.).

To some extent, this difference in salary suggests discrimination against women workers. As the Women's Bureau points out, it may not ". . . necessarily indicate that women are receiving unequal pay for equal work." Instead, it indicates ". . . that women are more likely than men to be employed in low-skilled, low-paying jobs."

In public elementary and secondary schools, women were less than 20 percent of the principals; superintendents; deputy, associate, and assistant superintendents; and other central office administrators in 1970–71.

Among professional and technical workers in business, women are concentrated in the class B and class C computer programer positions, while men are more frequently employed in the higher paying class A positions. Similarly, women are usually in the lowest category of draftsmen and engineering technicians.

Among managers and proprietors, women frequently operate small retail establishments, while men may manage manufacturing plants or wholesale outlets. In the manufacturing of men's and boys' suits and coats, women are likely to be employed as hand finishers, thread trimmers and basting pullers, and sewing machine operators — jobs where their average hourly earnings are less than $2.70 — while men are likely to be employed as finish pressers (hand or machine), underpressers, cutters, and markers — with average hourly earnings of $3.50 to $4.25.

In the service occupations, women are likely to be cooks, nurses' aides, and waitresses, while men are likely to be employed in higher paying jobs as bartenders, guards, custodians, firemen, policemen, and detectives.

Yet, as the Women's Bureau report on the earnings gap makes clear:

> . . . within some of these detailed occupations, men usually are better paid. For example, Bureau of Labor Statistics surveys of earnings in major office occupations showed that during the period July 1969 to June 1970 men's average weekly earnings were substantially higher than those of women among class A and class B accounting and payroll clerks. The weekly salary differentials between women and men class A accounting clerks ranged from $6.50 to $42.50 in 60 of the important centers of business and industry surveyed.

The difference in earnings between men and women workers seems to be decreasing. In November 1970, the Women's Bureau surveyed the jobs and salaries to be offered by 191 companies to June 1971 college graduates. Although "Salaries to be offered to women were consistently below those to be offered to men with the same college major," the Bureau found that a comparison with 1970 showed ". . . a marked reduction in the spread between salaries for women and men. For 1970 the monthly gap ranged from $86 down to $18; for 1971 the gap ranged from $68 down to only $1 in engineering."

What do you think are the reasons for the reduction in the earnings gap? Why hasn't it been eliminated completely?

### Minority Group Women

The information given above deals with the position of women in general. But no discussion of women can be complete without at least a brief indication of the position of minority group women, 92 percent of whom are black. They form a distinct sub-group which may be the object of prejudice because of race as well as because of sex.

Minority group women are more likely to work than white women. According to the Department of Labor, for instance, in 1971 49 percent of black women worked while only 42 percent of white women did so. Nevertheless, minority group women are likely to be not as well educated as white women. In Table 7, compare the years of school completed by black and white women in 1970.

Perhaps because of the differences in educational achievement, the employment picture of minority group women is not the same as that for white women. Compare, for example, the occupation groups shown in Table 8.

In addition, the unemployment rate for minority group women tends to be greater than it is for women in general. The Department of Labor reported that in March 1971, for example, at the height of the recent recession, the percentage of unemployed women was 6.8, but the percentage for minority group women was much higher — 10.3.

The average income for minority group women, particularly blacks, is also lower than it is for white women. According to the Bureau of the Census, in 1970, the median income for white women was $5,427, but for nonwhites it was only $2,151.

To some extent, differences in employment and salaries can be explained by differences in educational levels. For the highly educated minority group woman, the employment picture seems very bright. In a special study on "The Social and Economic Status of Negroes in the United States, 1970," prepared jointly by the Bureau of the Census and the Bureau of Labor Statistics, it was found that "Negro women who had completed 4 years of college made sharper gains in income than the comparable group of white women. The median income of Negro women who had completed college was about $1,000 more than for white women with the same educational attainment."

Why do you think this occurred?

Table 7. Years of School Completed by Race in 1970

| Race | Persons 25 years old and over (1,000) | Years of school completed (percent distribution)* | | | | | | |
|---|---|---|---|---|---|---|---|---|
| | | Elementary school | | | High school | | College | |
| | | 0–4 years | 5–7 years | 8 years | 1–3 years | 4 years | 1–3 years | 4 or more years |
| White | 51,506 | 3.9 | 7.8 | 13.4 | 17.3 | 39.0 | 10.1 | 8.6 |
| Black | 5,470 | 12.1 | 17.3 | 11.3 | 24.5 | 24.4 | 6.0 | 4.4 |

*Source:* Statistical Abstracts, 1971.
* Median values are 12.2 years of school completed for whites and 10.2 for blacks.

Table 8. Occupation of Employed Women 18 Years Old and Over by Color and Years of School Completed in the United States for May 1969

| Color and occupation | Total employed (in thousands) | Median school years completed |
|---|---|---|
| White | | |
| Total, all occupation groups | 24,291 | 12.4 |
| Professional, technical, and kindred workers | 3,180 | 16.4 |
| Managers, officials, and proprietors, except farm | 1,166 | 12.5 |
| Clerical workers | 8,870 | 12.6 |
| Salesworkers | 1,709 | 12.3 |
| Craftsmen, operatives, laborers, except farm and mine | 4,035 | 10.8 |
| Private household workers | 704 | 9.8 |
| Service workers except private household | 3,602 | 12.0 |
| Farmers, farm managers, laborers and foremen | 395 | 11.4 |
| Nonwhite | | |
| Total, all occupation groups | 3,446 | 11.9 |
| Professional and managerial workers* | 424 | 16.2 |
| Clerical and sales workers | 741 | 12.6 |
| Craftsmen, operatives, and laborers, except farm and mine | 664 | 11.2 |
| Private household workers | 702 | 8.4 |
| Service workers, except private household | 885 | 10.9 |
| Farmers, farm managers, laborers, and foremen | 30 | † |

*Source:* Department of Health, Education, and Welfare, Digest of Educational Statistics, 1970.
* Includes persons reporting no school years completed.
† Percentage not shown where base is less than 75,000.

## Federal Legislation

The position of women as workers looks more encouraging for the future because of Federal legislation on sex discrimination passed in the 1960s. The major acts and order are:

### The Equal Pay Act of 1963

This act, which became generally effective on June 11, 1964, is an amendment to the Fair Labor Standards Act passed in 1938. According to the Women's Bureau, the act:

... prohibits discrimination on the basis of sex in the payment of wages for equal work on jobs that require equal skill, effort, and responsibility, and that are performed under similar working conditions. Its provisions apply to "wages" in the sense of remuneration for employment (including overtime) and to employer contributions for most fringe benefits. In a landmark decision, a Federal court held that women performing work which is "substantially" equal to that of men should receive the same pay. The Supreme Court denied review. The act is enforced by the Department of Labor.*

### Title VII of the Civil Rights Act of 1964, as amended by the Equal Employment Opportunity Act of 1972

Title VII is a landmark in the struggle for equal rights for women. According to the Women's Bureau, it

... prohibits discrimination on the basis of sex, as well as on race, color, religion, and national origin, by employers of 25 or more employees, . . . public and private employment agencies, labor unions, and labor-management apprenticeship programs. State and local government agencies and public and private educational institutions are newly covered, but religious educational institutions or associations are exempt with respect to the employment of individuals of a particular religion. Employers excluded from coverage are Federal and District of Columbia agencies

* This quote and those following are from "Brief Highlights on Major Laws and Orders on Sex Discrimination," Women's Bureau, Department of Labor.

(other than the Federal-State employment service system), federally owned corporations, and Indian tribes. Specifically excluded from the definition of "employee" are State and local elected officials and their personal staff and policy-making appointees.

Discrimination based on race, color, sex, religion, or national origin is unlawful in hiring or firing; wages; fringe benefits; classifying, referring, assigning, or promoting employees; extending or assigning use of facilities; training, retraining, or apprenticeships; or any other terms, conditions, or privileges of employment.

The Equal Employment Opportunity Commission (EEOC), which enforces title VII, has issued "Guidelines on Discrimination Because of Sex." The guidelines bar hiring based on stereotyped characterization of the sexes, classifications or labeling of "men's jobs" and "women's jobs," or advertising under male or female headings. They specify that the bona fide occupational qualification exemption should be interpreted narrowly, and that State laws which prohibit or limit the employment of women — in certain occupations considered hazardous or in jobs that require lifting or carrying weights in excess of prescribed limits, working during certain hours of the night, or working more than a specified number of hours per day or per week — conflict with and are superseded by title VII. Accordingly, these "protective" labor laws cannot be used as a reason for refusing to employ women.

Revised guidelines, issued April 5, 1972, include a provision that, where State laws require minimum wage and overtime pay for women only, an employer not only may not refuse to hire female applicants to avoid this payment but must provide the same benefits for male employees. Similar provisions apply to rest and meal periods and physical facilities, although if an employer can prove that business necessity precludes providing these benefits to both men and women, the employer need not provide them to members of either sex.

The revised guidelines prohibit excluding from employment an applicant or employee because of pregnancy. They state, among other things, that disabilities caused or contributed to by pregnancy, miscarriage, abortion, childbirth, and recovery therefrom are, for all job-related purposes, temporary disabilities and should be treated as such under any health or temporary disability insurance or sick leave plan available in connection with employment. Accrual of seniority, reinstatement, and payment under such insurance or plan should therefore be applied to disability due to pregnancy or childbirth as to other temporary disabilities.

*Executive Order 11246, as amended* (effective October 14, 1968)

As the Women's Bureau points out, this Order

. . . prohibits employment discrimination based on sex, as well as on race, color, religion, or national origin, by Federal contractors or subcontractors and contractors who perform work under a federally assisted construction contract exceeding $10,000. Coverage includes all facilities of the contractor, regardless of whether they are involved in the performance of the Federal contract. The order does not exempt specific kinds of employment or employees.

Prohibited practices include discrimination in recruitment or recruitment advertising; hiring, upgrading, demotion, or transfer; layoff or termination; rates of pay or other compensation; and selection for training, including apprenticeship.

The Office of Federal Contract Compliance (OFCC), which enforces the order, has issued "Sex Discrimination Guidelines." The guidelines state, among other things, that contractors may not advertise under male and female classifications, base seniority lists on sex, deny a person a job because of State "protective" labor laws, make distinctions between married and unmarried persons of one sex only, or penalize women in their terms and conditions of employment because they require leave for childbearing. The guidelines also specifically require the granting of a leave of absence to an employee for childbearing and reinstatement to her original job or to a position of like status and pay, without loss of service credits.

The effect of these acts and orders are just beginning to be felt. How do you think they will change the following:

• Women's salaries?
• Women's jobs?
• Women's education?
• Traditional concepts of sexual roles?

# Chapter 3

# Women's Social

# and Civil Status

The renaissance of the women's rights movement, which began during the 1960s, has renewed interest in all areas relating to women. The movement is attempting to change not only woman's position as worker but, as well, her position as a member of American society.

We turn now to the social and civil issues which many people consider to be the major ones in the struggle for women's rights. As these are raised, ask yourself whether you consider them significant and decide how you think they affect the position of women in society.

## Discrimination

We have seen that women are less likely to be as well educated as men, apt to do different work, and to receive lower salaries. There are additional indications that women in the United States are not treated as the equals of men.

*Law*

In a 1970 memorandum on the Equal Rights Amendment, the Citizens' Advisory Council on the Status of Women argued that discrimination against women exists in laws which "distinguish on the basis of sex." The kinds of laws they found discriminatory are:

1. State laws placing special restrictions on women with respect to hours of work and weightlifting on the job;

2. State laws prohibiting women from working in certain occupations;

3. Laws or practices operating to exclude women from State colleges and universities (including higher standards required for women applicants to institutions of higher learning and in the administration of scholarship programs);

4. Discrimination in employment in State and local governments;

5. Dual pay schedules for men and women public school teachers;

6. State laws providing for alimony to be awarded, under certain circumstances, to ex-wives but not to ex-husbands;

7. State laws placing special restrictions on the legal capacity of married women or on their right to establish a legal domicile;

8. State laws that require married women but not married men to go through a formal procedure and obtain court approval before they may engage in an independent business;

9. Social Security and other social benefits legislation which give greater benefits to one sex than to the other;

10. Discriminatory preferences, based on sex, in child custody cases;

11. State laws providing that the *father* is the natural guardian of the minor children;

12. Different ages for males and females in (a) child labor laws, (b) age for marriage, (c) cutoff of the right to parental support, and (d) juvenile court jurisdiction;

13. Exclusion of women from the requirements of the Military Selective Service Act of 1967;

14. Special sex-based exemptions for women in selection of State juries;

15. Heavier criminal penalties for female offenders than for male offenders committing the same crime.

Which of these laws seem to protect women rather than discriminate against them? Should women be protected legally?

*Housing*

Housing appears to be another area in which there is evidence of discrimination against women. Let us look, for instance, at the problem as it exists in New York City. Because it is a large metropolis which has a varied ethnic population and numerous transients, one might assume that New York is an open city in which a woman is free to live anywhere she chooses. According to the Hearings of the New York City Commission on Human Rights, held in September 1970, this is not the case. Carol Greitzer, a member of the City Council, testified that, "Figures compiled by private rental agencies note the high rate of discrimination against women in the East 50s, 60s, and 70s, particularly along the Lexington-Third Avenue axis, possibly because many men find this a desirable neighborhood. . . ." Carter Burden, another member of the Council, testified and supported her findings:

> It is an incontestable fact that in both private and public housing there is severe discrimination against unmarried women under 62 years old, including Mitchell-Lama middle-incoming housing. One of my constituents has applied for nearly every middle-income housing development over the past 15 years. Each time she is near the top of the list of applicants, and each time she is called in for an interview, and each time she is told that she qualifies for the apartment which she seeks, but that because of her *age* and lack of *marital status*, she will be denied an apartment (despite the rather ironic fact that she contributes an inordinately large percentage of her income to the taxes used to create that development because she is unmarried).

*Public Accommodation*

In addition, the Hearings suggest that in places of public accommodation, there is also some evidence that women are treated differently than men. George Zuckerman, an Assistant Attorney-General for New York State, testified:

> Some of the most humiliating experiences that have been encountered by women have resulted from the refusal of hotels, nightclubs, cocktail lounges and even first-class

restaurants in New York City to admit women when un-escorted by a male. Several women have testified in our office that managers of nightclubs and restaurants advise them that if they return accompanied by a male they could gain admission. It is, thus, bitterly ironic that many of these female-exclusionary practices, which are defended on the grounds of public morality, would, in the words of these women, seem to encourage soliciting of male customers by females seeking to gain admission.

Why do you think women might have difficulty finding housing and going freely to places open to the general public?

*Public Life*

Finally, the question of discrimination arises when we consider the extent to which women are represented in the national political life of the country. Here is the record; no woman has ever been:

1. President of the United States. Although the names of a few have been placed in nomination (for example, Margaret Chase Smith and Shirley Chisholm), none has ever been a major party candidate for the Presidency.
2. Vice President
3. A member of the Supreme Court
4. Postmaster General
5. Attorney General
6. Secretary of State
7. Secretary of the Treasury
8. Secretary of Defense
9. Secretary of the Interior
10. Secretary of Agriculture
11. Secretary of Commerce
12. Secretary of Transportation
13. Secretary of Housing and Urban Development

In fact, only two women have ever held cabinet posts: Frances Perkins was Secretary of Labor from 1933 to 1945, and Oveta Culp Hobby was Secretary of the Department of Health, Education, and Welfare from 1953 to 1955.

In the 92nd Congress, only one woman, Margaret Chase Smith of Maine, was a member of the Senate. Only 12 women (three Republicans and nine Democrats) were in the House of Representatives.

How do you explain women's lack of participation?

## Marriage

Frequently women enter into marriage without realizing that as they take their vows, their legal status changes. Perhaps the most obvious symbol of that change is a woman's name. Whether married or single, a man's surname never alters. But when a woman marries, she drops the name she was born with and takes on her husband's. What do you think this change represents for the wife?

Some of the legal responsibilities of husband and wife are discussed in the following paragraphs. As you read them, ask yourself what these laws tell you about society's attitudes toward marriage as a contract between two people.

A husband must support his wife. However, as the Citizens' Advisory Council on the Status of Women states in its 1971 report to the President of the United States, "The rights to support of women and children are much more limited than is generally known and enforcement is very inadequate. A married woman living with her husband can in practice get only what he chooses to give her."

In turn, as Daniel J. DeBenedictis points out in *Legal Rights of Married Women*, " . . . if the husband becomes physically or mentally incapacitated, the burden of support for the husband and the children falls upon the wife."

Moreover, a wife is required to keep house for her husband. Whether or not she works outside the home, she is responsible for making certain that the household runs efficiently, either by doing the work herself or by hiring servants.

If her husband changes his job or is transferred, as Mr. DeBenedictis explains, a wife must follow him " . . . whenever he chooses to work at a reasonable job in a reasonable location." In other words, unless there are unusual circumstances and whether or not a wife wishes to leave the place in which she lives, she is legally required to do so.

As Mr. DeBenedictis states, a wife " . . . does not have to work in her husband's business, any more than she has to work at all. However, if she works for her husband she cannot demand a salary because her work would be in the nature of the wife's services to which a husband is already legally entitled." Thus, a woman who works at two full-time jobs — as a housewife and an employee in her husband's business — can still be without funds of her own and totally dependent upon the money her husband gives her.

Finally, in marriage, as Mr. DeBenedictis makes clear, "The husband is always entitled to the exclusive sexual relations and services of his wife." However, the wife " . . . has no legal obligation to bear and rear children for her husband."

If a couple is divorced, the wife is legally entitled to alimony. The Citizens' Advisory Council on the Status of Women, however, pointed out in its 1971 report that the only national study of alimony and child support (made by the American Bar Association in 1965), indicates that " . . . alimony is awarded in a very small percentage of cases."

The Citizens' Advisory Council also reported that, "With respect to child support, the data available indicates that payments generally are less than enough to furnish half of the support of the children." As a result, many divorced women are forced to work to support their children. According to the Council, "With the earnings of women averaging 60 percent those of men, women who work to support their children are contributing by and large more than their proportionate share, even when fathers comply fully with awards."

What is your reaction to these legal responsibilities? Do you think they are fair to women? Are they fair to men?

## Birth Control

The question of whether or not we should control population through controlling the number of births has become an important issue in the 1970s, as we have come to realize that the earth — our home — cannot continue to support increasing numbers of human beings. The Commission on Population Growth and the American Future emphasizes the seriousness of the problem in its 1972 report to the President and the Congress, *Population and the American Future*. The Commission stated that even small-sized families will add enormously to the population.

> One hundred years from now, the 2-child family would result in a population of about 350 million persons, whereas, the 3-child family would produce a total of nearly a billion. . . . Thus, a difference of only one extra child per family

would result in an additional 51 million people over the next three decades, and if extended over a century, an additional two-thirds of a billion people.

The Commission suggested that if the rate of population growth is slowed, the quality of life in the United States would improve. For example, the "average person will be markedly better off in terms of traditional economic values," resources and the environment will be conserved, the nation will have time to devote its attentions to the "quality of life rather than its quantity," and there will be "reduced pressures on educational and other services."

Many people accept the Commission's conclusion that population growth in the United States must be slowed. Some form of birth control seems to offer the best solution.

The three most effective methods of birth control are: voluntary sterilization, the use of contraceptives, and abortion. Let us examine the social attitudes toward each.

## Voluntary Sterilization

Of the three, voluntary sterilization has caused the least controversy, although its use as a method of birth control is becoming more prevalent. The Commission on Population reports that a 1970 National Fertility Study undertaken by the Office of Population Research at Princeton University found that almost three million spouses, that is, approximately one couple in five, had undergone sterilization operations. Unlike the use of contraceptives and abortion, there are few legal problems to face.

## The Use of Contraceptives

The use of contraceptives to prevent pregnancy has often met with resistance. For example, it was not until 1971 that Congress repealed the 1873 Comstock Act, which, as the Commission on Population explains, prohibited " . . . the importation, transportation in interstate commerce, and mailing of 'any article whatever for the prevention of conception.'" According to the Commission, as of 1972:

> Approximately 22 states prohibit the sale of all or some contraceptives; but all states, either by statute or common law, allow exceptions for doctors, pharmacists, or other licensed firms or individuals. Roughly 23 states prohibit

commercial advertising of contraceptives, but most of these states make exceptions for medical and pharmaceutical journals.

The same 23 states also condemn the display of contraceptives and of information about them, but, with a few possible exceptions, explicitly permit such display under certain circumstances. At least 27 states, either expressly or inferentially, prohibit the sale of contraceptives through vending machines.

Literal interpretations of these anti-birth control laws are often unreliable; their enforcement is uneven, and in some instances, there are conflicting interpretations. In some states, court decisions have modified or even nullified the letter of the statue.

Social and legal attitudes toward the use of contraceptives, therefore, often seem to be in conflict.

If population growth is to be slowed, existing antibirth control statues regarding contraceptives would have to be repealed. In addition, education in family planning would probably have to become more widespread since a large number of births are now unplanned. The survey conducted by the Office of Population Research indicated, for example, that of the married women who became pregnant from 1966 to 1970, 44 percent had not intended to have a child and 15 percent did not want one.

Do you think more effort and money should be spent to educate people about family planning and the use of contraceptives? Who should be educated?

*Abortion*

Attempts to legalize abortion have aroused enormous controversy, despite the fact that illegal abortions have been frequent. According to the Commission on Population, it is estimated that anywhere from 200,000 to 1,200,000 take place each year in the United States. Yet social and legal attitudes toward abortion change slowly, if at all.

As the Commission points out in its 1972 report, abortion continued to be illegal in over two-thirds of the states:

> . . . except to preserve the life of the mother; 12 states have changed their abortion statutes consistent with the American Law Institute Model Penal Code provision on abortion

which prohibits abortion except in cases where the mother's life or her mental or physical health is in danger, or to prevent the birth of defective offspring, or in cases of rape or incest.

In 1970 liberalized abortion laws were passed by the legislatures of Alaska, Hawaii and New York and by popular referendum in Washington. But even in these states the issue was not resolved. In New York, for instance, the law passed in 1970 gave women the right to legal abortion within the first 24 weeks of pregnancy. In 1972, the legislature voted to repeal this law. It remained in effect only because the Governor vetoed the new bill when it reached his desk.

A United States Supreme Court decision announced in January 1973, declared that state laws which restricted the right to abortion under medically safe conditions within the first 24 weeks of pregnancy were unconstitutional. This did not abolish all abortion laws, but it limits states to only permit laws affecting abortion after 24 weeks.

For most people, the question of abortion is controversial because it raises moral or religious issues. For some, abortion opposes their religious beliefs and teachings. For others, it represents a violation of the sanctity of human life, which begins at the moment of inception. For still others, abortion is simply murder; to abort a fetus, they argue, is to kill a human being. For those women involved in the struggle to legalize abortion, however, it is a personal decision, one which every woman has the right to make for herself. What do you think?

The problems of population growth and birth control have significant implications for women. It is, after all, women who bear and usually rear children. Any discussion of birth control, therefore, raises questions about the degree to which each woman has the right to control her own body, and the extent to which society has the right to decide for her. In addition, if population growth is slowed, which seems likely, increasing numbers of women will have few or no children. As a result, less of their time and energy will be needed to bear and bring up children, and much more will be available for other activities. The consequences of this change are unknown. We can only wonder:

- What will women do?
- How will their role and position in society be affected?
- What will be the impact upon men? Upon society?

## Child Care Services

The issue of child care services is both economic and social. It is economic because the number of working mothers continues to increase. The Bureau of Labor Statistics reported that as of March 1970, for example, 39.8 percent of working wives had children under 18 and 39.3 percent had children under six. In addition, the Department of Labor projects that by 1985, there will be as many as 6.6 million working mothers with children under five, representing an expected increase of 32 percent within the ten year period between 1975 and 1985.

It is a social issue for the following reasons. First, according to many involved in the women's rights movement, the existence of adequate child care services gives women the opportunity to control their time, thus permitting them to pursue their own interests rather than devoting almost all of their time to caring for others. Second, the existence of such services can determine the social and economic level at which a family lives. In 1972, the Women's Bureau reported that 14 percent of the families in which the wife does not work live in poverty, while in those families where the wife works only 4 percent live in poverty. In other words, a working mother usually means a higher standard of living for the family, better housing, food, clothing, and medical care for her children. Third, the kind of care available for the children of working mothers, particularly during the important first six years of a child's life, affects the development of the child's personality and, perhaps, his educational potential as well. Fourth, the question of whether child care services should be financed and developed completely by the Federal government as a free public service brings up the possibility of excessive government control in the raising of children and ultimately, perhaps, the creation of the kind of authoritarian society George Orwell describes in *1984*. Last, the rearing of large numbers of children in group child care centers presents a dramatic change in the pattern of American life. Traditionally, child care has been the primary responsibility of the mother. No one knows what the effect will be if numerous children spend most of their day in group care centers rather than with members of their family.

At present, child care services take a variety of forms. In 1970, the Women's Bureau found:

> Less than half of the preschool children were cared for in their homes; not quite a third, in someone else's home; a

little more than 5 percent, in group care centers; and the remainder, under other arrangements. Some were cared for by their mother while she worked; others — "latchkey children" — cared for themselves.

But child care services are pitifully inadequate for the demand. The Women's Bureau found that, "According to the latest estimates [made by the Department of Health, Education and Welfare in 1969], day care in licensed centers and family homes is available for only about 640,000 children. It is estimated that several million children need this service."

Group child care centers have been established by some private companies, as, for example, KLH Research and Development Corporation, Skyland Textile Company, and Avco Printing Plant. Some companies serve their employees only; others, like KLH and Avco, provide services for children in the community as well. In addition, the Women's Bureau found that as of 1970, 114 hospitals provided group child care services for their health personnel. Universities, women's groups, and community groups — along with State agencies — also provide such services. But the number of group child care centers does not meet the need.

Do you think that all private companies should be required to open group child care centers for their employees? Or do you think the responsibility for child care services of all kinds should lay with the parents, the community, the city, the state, or the Federal government?

Thus far, the Federal government has been involved in child care only to a limited degree.

Some funds for services are available under a number of acts. For example, according to the Women's Bureau, The Economic Opportunity Act ". . . authorizes grants for the development, conduct, and administration of day care projects within community action programs." The Elementary and Secondary Education Act of 1965 provides funds for "educationally deprived" children. The Vocational Education Act of 1963, which authorizes funds to provide training in home economics occupations, may, according to the Women's Bureau, ". . . include training of aides and assistants to directors of day care centers." As the Bureau points out, The Education Professions Development Act ". . . provides funds for the training and retraining of personnel who serve youngsters in preschool programs, day care centers, kindergartens, and in the early years of the elementary school."

In 1968, at the request of the President, the Secretary of the

Department of Health, Education, and Welfare established the Federal Panel on Early Childhood, which was composed of representatives from all Federal agencies concerned with the family and children. The purpose of the Panel is to improve all childhood programs financed by Federal funds. It has developed standards which, according to the Women's Bureau, ". . . apply to all major federally assisted day care programs and establish minimum requirements for facilities; education, social, health, and nutrition services; staff training; parent involvement; administration; coordination; and evaluation." In addition, it has drawn up a plan, called the Community Coordinated Child Care Program, ". . . to coordinate all programs that provide services to children and their families at all levels of operation."

The Revenue Act of 1971 liberalized tax deductions for child care expenses. Praising the passage of the law, President Nixon stated that the deductions:

> . . . will provide a significant Federal subsidy for day care in families where both parents are employed, potentially benefiting 97 percent of all such families in the country and offering parents free choice of the child care arrangements they deem best for their families. This approach reflects my conviction that the Federal Government's role wherever possible should be one of assisting parents to purchase needed day care services in the private, open market, with Federal involvement in direct provision of such services kept to an absolute minimum.

Not all Federal legislators agree that the government's involvement in child care services should be as limited as the President suggested. The Comprehensive Child Development Act of 1971, which would have established child development centers in every community, was part of an anti-poverty bill passed by both Houses of Congress. It would have become law if it had not been vetoed by President Nixon. As quoted in the April 30, 1972 *New York Times Magazine* article on day care centers by William V. Shannon, the President did so because:

> All other factors being equal, good public policy requires that we enhance rather than diminish both parental authority and parental involvement with children — particularly in those decisive early years when social attitudes and a conscience are formed, and religious and moral principles are first inculcated.

Nevertheless, it is probable that the government's involvement in child care services will increase. As William Shannon points out when writing about the child development plan, "The political arithmetic of the growing number of working mothers guarantees that."

Recognizing that the demand for child care services will continue to develop, the Commission on Population recommended:

> . . . both public and private forces join together to assure that adequate child-care services, including health, nutritional, and educational components, are available to families who wish to make use of them.

> *Because child-care programs represent a major innovation in child-rearing in this country, we recommend that continuing research and evaluation be undertaken to determine the benefits and costs to children, parents, and the public of alternative child-care arrangements.*

Do these recommendations offer adequate solutions to the problem of child care? How do you think the demand for child care services can be met so that the needs of children, women, and society are fulfilled?

## Poverty

No discussion concerned with the status of women can ignore the fact that poverty is a way of life for a large number of them. According to the Women's Bureau, in 1970 at least 10 percent of the families in the United States were living in poverty, that is, they were living on less than $2,525 a year for a couple, or $3,968 for a family of four. Of these families, 8 percent were white, 29 percent were black, and 14 percent belong to other minority groups.

The Bureau reported that although in general the number of poor families is decreasing, "The sex of the family head is an increasingly important factor in the poverty status of families."

> About 1 out of every 3 families headed by a woman lived in poverty in 1970 as compared with 1 out of 14 families headed by a man. The poverty rate was highest among

Negro families headed by a woman — 54 percent, more than double the 25 percent for white families headed by a woman. The proportions for Negro and white families headed by a man were 18 and 6 percent, respectively.

Compare, for example, the statistics given in Table 9.

Table 9.  Poor Families in 1970

| Type of family | Number (in millions) | | | As percent of all families | | |
|---|---|---|---|---|---|---|
| | All races | White | Negro | All races | White | Negro |
| Total | 5.2 | 3.7 | 1.4 | 10.0 | 8.0 | 29.3 |
| Male head | 3.3 | 2.6 | .6 | 7.1 | 6.2 | 18.3 |
| Female head | 1.9 | 1.1 | .9 | 32.5 | 25.0 | 54.5 |

*Source:* Women's Bureau, Fact Sheet on the American Family in Poverty, 1971 (rev.).

Table 10.  Children Under 18 Living in Poverty in 1970

| Type of family | Number (in millions) | | | As percent of all children under 18 | | |
|---|---|---|---|---|---|---|
| | All races | White | Negro | All races | White | Negro |
| Total | 10.5 | 6.2 | 4.1 | 15.0 | 10.5 | 41.5 |
| Male head | 5.7 | 3.9 | 1.6 | 9.3 | 7.3 | 26.0 |
| Female head | 4.8 | 2.3 | 2.5 | 53.4 | 43.2 | 67.9 |

*Source:* Women's Bureau, Fact Sheet on the American Family in Poverty, 1971 (rev.).

Without doubt, the number of children living in poverty is affected to a large extent by the sex of the parent who provides support. The Bureau found that in 1970, 15 percent of all children under 18 were poor. Of these, 11 percent were white and 42 percent were black. However, as Table 10 makes clear, "The incidence of poverty among children was highest (68 percent) in Negro families headed by a woman."

Furthermore, it is worth noting that, as Jack Goldberg, Commissioner of the New York City Social Services, pointed out at the 1970 Hearings of the Commission on Human Rights:

. . . The overwhelming majority of persons on public assist-
ance in this country [that is, on welfare] are in fact female-
headed households, what we call in our jargon the "ADC
families," Aid to Dependent Children families.

In his testimony, he described the position of the welfare mother:

. . . the woman who is a welfare mother is the victim of all
of our society and policies and lack of addressing ourselves
to the problems that this situation represents. It represents,
I think, the ultimate in deprivation as a human being — not
just in women's rights terms but just the ultimate deprivation as a human being; not having the opportunity to be a
whole family; living on inadequate levels; not having the
option of going to work because there are no child care
facilities; and becoming the object of coercive work in the
most undignified and inappropriate terms.

Do you agree? Considering the position of women in the
United States today, can you explain why so many families
headed by women are living in poverty or on welfare?

### The Equal Rights Amendment

The Equal Rights Amendment is the most significant action
taken to improve the status of women in the United States since
1920, when the ratification of the Nineteenth Amendment gave
women the right to vote. The Amendment reads as follows:

*Resolved by the Senate and House of Representatives of
the United States of America in Congress assembled (two-
thirds of each House concurring therein),* That the following
article is proposed as an amendment to the Constitution of
the United States, which shall be valid to all intents and
purposes as part of the Constitution when ratified by the
legislatures of three-fourths of the several States within
seven years from the date of its submission by the Congress:

"Article —

Section 1. Equality of rights under the law shall not be
denied or abridged by the United States or by any State on
account of sex.

Section 2. The Congress shall have the power to enforce, by
appropriate legislation, the provisions of this article.

**Section 3.** This amendment shall take effect two years after the date of ratification."

After a struggle of more than fifty years, an Equal Rights Amendment was passed by Congress. It was first passed in the House of Representatives on October 12, 1971, by a vote of 354 to 23. On March 22, 1972, it was passed in the Senate by a vote of 84 to 8. Once the Amendment is approved by 38 states, sexual equality becomes one of the legal rights guaranteed by the Constitution. According to the Senate Committee on the Judiciary, the Equal Rights Amendment is necessary.

While there has been some progress towards the goal of equal rights and responsibilities for men and women in recent years, there is overwhelming evidence that persistent patterns of sex discrimination permeate our social, cultural, and economic life. The magnitude of sex discrimination in the country today can be gauged by the simple and eloquent statement of Congresswoman Shirley Chisolm when she testified before the Subcommittee on Constitutional Amendments in May 1970: "I have been far oftener discriminated against because I am a woman than because I am black."

The passage of the Equal Rights Amendment in Congress did not occur without controversy. As the votes cited above illustrate, not everyone was in favor of the Amendment. The major reasons for opposing it were:

- It is unnecessary. The Equal Rights Clause of the Fourteenth Amendment covers most of the areas of discrimination.
- Changes in inequitable laws should be handled by State legislatures and in the courts.
- Some discrimination benefits women. For example, the hours women can work are limited by law. Women are protected from lifting heavy weights.
- If the Amendment passed, women would become eligible for military service and even combat duty.
- Differences in criminal laws, some of which benefit women, would be abolished.
- Marriage laws — which define the responsibilities of both husband and wife — would be altered. As a result, the Equal Rights Amendment endangers the traditional structure of the American family.

- The Amendment threatens the entire American social structure because it ignores the biological differences between the sexes. For example, as quoted in the "Report of the Senate Committee on the Judiciary," Senator Sam Ervin argued:

> The physiological and functional differences between men and women empower men to beget and women to bear children, who enter life in a state of utter helplessness and ignorance, and who must receive nurture, care, and training at the hands of adults throughout their early years if they and the race are to survive, and if they are to grow mentally and spiritually. From time whereof the memory of mankind runneth not to the contrary, custom and law have imposed upon men the primary responsibility for providing a habitation and a livelihood for their wives and children to enable their wives to make the habitations homes, and to furnish nurture, care, and training to their children during their early years.
>
> In this respect, custom and law reflect the wisdom embodied in the ancient Yiddish proverb that God could not be everywhere, so he made mothers. The physiological and functional differences between men and women constitute the most important reality. Without them human life could not exist.
>
> For this reason, any country which ignores these differences when it fashions its institutions and makes its laws is woefully lacking in rationality.

Those who supported the passage of the Equal Rights Amendment responded as follows:

- The Fourteenth Amendment is inadequate. As the Senate Report points out, for example, the Supreme Court does ". . . not hold that sex discrimination is 'suspect' under the Fourteenth Amendment."
- Changes through state legislatures and courts are too slow and uncertain. For instance, according to the Senate Report, in 1972, "In the States, progress has been mixed. Some States have made diligent efforts to revise outmoded and discriminatory laws, and three States — Illinois, Pennsylvania and Virginia — have recently approved State constitutional provisions banning sex discrimination. But in other States, there has been no progress at all." In the courts, without the

Equal Rights Amendment, the burden would be "on each woman plaintiff to show sex discrimination is 'unreasonable.' "

- Discrimination is often more detrimental than beneficial, and laws which supposedly "protect" women in fact usually stop them from achieving equal opportunities. As the Senate Report states, for example, " . . . a law which limits the working hours of women but not of men makes it more difficult for women to obtain work they desire and for which they are qualified, or to become supervisors. State laws which limit the amount of weight a woman can lift or carry arbitrarily keep all women from certain desirable or high-paying jobs, although many if not most women are fully capable of performing the tasks required."
- Under the Equal Rights Amendment, women will be able to volunteer for military service as men do. According to the Senate Report:

  This result is highly desirable for today women are often arbitrarily barred from military service and from the benefits which flow from it: for example, educational benefits of the G.I. bill; medical care in the service and through Veterans Hospitals; job preferences in government and out; and the training, maturity and leadership provided by service in the military itself.

If there is a draft, men and women will probably be treated equally.

- For those crimes which are committed by both sexes, the law will punish the offenders on the basis of the nature of the crime, not on the basis of sex. The Equal Rights Amendment, however, will not invalidate sex crimes such as rape.
- The Equal Rights Amendment eliminates marriage laws which discriminate on the basis of sex. Consequently, according to the Senate Report, laws " . . . will have to be based on individual circumstances and needs and not on sexual stereotypes." As the Association of the Bar of the City of New York points out, the Amendment prevents:

  . . . a state from imposing a greater liability on one spouse than on the other merely because of sex. It is clear that the Amendment would not require both a husband and wife to contribute identical amounts of money to a marriage. The support obligation of each spouse would be defined in functional terms based, for example, on each spouse's earning power, current resources and nonmonetary contributions to the family welfare.

- The Equal Rights Amendment improves the American social structure by requiring that, as the Senate Report states, " . . . the federal government and all state and local governments treat each person, male and female, as an individual." It " . . . applies only to governmental action; it does not affect the private action or the purely social relationships between men and women." Therefore, the problems raised by critics of the Equal Rights Amendment are not valid.

Although the Equal Rights Amendment deals only with women's legal rights, its full impact upon American society will not be felt for many years. No one really knows, for example, how it will change:

- Women's education
- Women's work
- Women's role as wife and mother
- Women's status in American society
- Women's psychology
- The cultural attitudes toward women
- The definition of a woman

What do you think?

# Chapter 4

# Views of Women

The attitudes which have created the position of women in the United States today derive from views of woman which are part of a long cultural and historical heritage. These views are often so much a part of the way we think that they seem "natural." We base our judgments on them, but we rarely question them, or even question the idea that perhaps we ought to question them.

The controversy aroused by the renaissance of the women's rights movement has brought about new interest in these views. Large numbers of men and women are beginning to take a hard look at them. They have begun to ask these questions:

- Are they true to my experience?
- How can I tell the difference between myth and reality?
- What can the past teach me and my children?

In this chapter we will examine major traditional views about the nature and role of woman. As you will discover, these views were not and are not accepted by everyone. Approach the arguments with an open mind, consider them, and decide for yourself whether or not they are worthwhile.

## VIEW: The Biological Differences between Man and Woman Result in Differences in Temperament and Behavior

According to this view, woman's temperament and behavior are innately different from man's, and her physical characteristics are indications of these differences. Because she is usually smaller and less muscular than man, she is often considered "the weaker sex." Her lack of physical strength may be taken as a sign, for example, that her will is weaker than man's, that her beliefs can be swayed more easily, and that her approach to life is more emotional or subjective. The Biblical account of Adam and Eve provides one illustration of this concept of woman. Eve ate the apple and thus brought misery to mankind not because she was evil but because she was so weak that she could be deceived by the serpent's words. In addition, great works of literature frequently reflect this same concept. For example, Shakespeare's Hamlet cries out, "Frailty, thy name is woman." And in his satirical "Moral Essays," Alexander Pope assumes woman to be so weak that:

"Most Women have no Characters at all."

Matter too soft a lasting mark to bear,
And best distinguished by black, brown, or fair.

A good deal of scientific and psychological theory supports the view that there is a biological explanation for sexual differences in temperament and behavior.

Experiments on animals suggest that sex hormones may account for such differences. According to an article on the relationship of sex hormones and behavior by Maggie Scarf (*The New York Times Magazine*, May 7, 1972), it was found in experiments on mice, for example, that ". . . fighting among males commences with the onset of puberty, when hormone levels are rising abruptly. Female mice fight only rarely, as is the case for males which have been castrated." During experiments on monkeys, Dr. Robert Rose and his co-workers found that, "The higher a monkey's male hormone concentration was, the higher his position in the 'pecking order' tended to be."

In his lecture on "Femininity," Sigmund Freud, the founder of psychoanalysis, argued that the physical sexual differences between man and woman have a detrimental effect on woman's temperament. Woman, he believed, is envious of male genitals. As a result, according to Freud, women have ". . . little sense of justice . . ." because of a ". . . predominance of envy in their mental life; for the demand for justice is a modification of envy and lays down the condition subject to which one can put envy aside." In addition, he regarded ". . . women as weaker in their social interests and as having less capacity for sublimating their instincts then men."

The psychoanalyst Theodor Reik, whose books have been read widely, considered that woman was naturally different from man. He found her to be more subjective and more perceptive. In *Sex in Man and Woman*, basing his conclusions on his observations of his patients, he found, for example, that in married couples, ". . . the woman is not only more attentive to, and more aware of, the mood and its changes than the man — but also more perceptive in regard to it."

Anthony Storr, a British psychiatrist, concludes in *Human Aggression* that as in ". . . most of the higher species of animals . . ." in human beings, ". . . the male is more aggressive than the female." Consequently, differences in behavior are natural since, as he argues, "There is a biologically appropriate way for males to be aggressive and another for the female. . . . Although we happen to live in a culture and at a time when the roles of the sexes are somewhat ill-defined, it is still true to say that dominance and a touch of ruthlessness in a man are admired, whereas the same qualities manifested in a woman are generally deplored as unfeminine."

In *Men in Groups*, a study of ". . . the relationship between biology and sociology as sciences and between biological processes and social processes as realities . . .," Professor Lionel Tiger emphasizes the biological differences between man and woman and their effect upon social organization:

When a community deals with its most vital problems, when statements of internal and external importance are made, when — particularly in warfare — decisive action must be taken, at these times females do not participate. The public forum is a male forum.

It is men who dominate the public and private State Councils of the world; . . . there are few "Spokeswomen." Chance's notions about "attention structure" are particularly relevant here; females may simply not release "followership" behavior. The "look" of them may be wrong for encounters of high state and gravity.

According to Professor Tiger, ". . . that females only rarely dominate authority structures may reflect females' underlying inability — at the ethological level of 'pattern releasing' behavior — to affect the behavior of subordinates. However, this general handicap apparently can be overcome by those females who have obviously participated in the use of power through their closely related men. More than any other factor, this appears to lend efficaciousness to females' otherwise ineffective political efforts."

Therefore, he argues, that male domination results from the biological make up of the human species.

> Males dominate females in occupational and political spheres. This is a species-specific pattern and is associated with my other proposition: that males bond in a variety of situations involving power, force, crucial or dangerous work, and relations with their gods. They consciously and emotionally *exclude* females from these bonds. The significant notion here is that these broad patterns are biologically based, and that those variously different expressions of male dominance and male bonding in different communities are what one would expect from a species highly adaptable to its physical and social environments, and where learning is a crucial adaptive process.

Obviously, man and woman differ physically. This is indisputable. However, the effect of these biological differences upon temperament and behavior is not as certain as these theories of personality and social organization imply. Those who reject the theories and the view of woman they represent offer the following arguments.

First, it is questionable whether the results of experiments upon animals are useful in understanding human behavior. For example, how do we know that what is true of mice or monkeys is equally true of man? In her article "Psychology Constructs the Female," Naomi Weisstein argues that basing theories on experiments with animals poses problems in the observation and interpretation of significant behavior.

> When behaviors from lower primates are directly opposite to those of higher primates, or to those one expects of humans, they can be dismissed on evolutionary grounds — higher primates and/or humans grew out of that kid stuff. On the other hand, if the behavior of higher primates is counter to the behavior considered natural for humans, while the behavior of some lower primate is considered natural for humans, the higher primate behavior can be dismissed also on the grounds that it has diverged from an older, prototypical pattern. So either way, one can select those behaviors

one wants to prove as innate for humans. In addition, one does not know whether the sex-role behavior exhibited is dependent on the phylogenetic rank or on the environmental conditions (both physical and social) under which different species live.*

Second, a consideration of biological differences is only valid after the question of cultural conditioning has been answered. Until this is done, we cannot know what is innate and what is acquired. After a study of three primitive societies, the anthropologist Margaret Mead, for example, concluded in her book *Sex and Temperament*:

> ... many, if not all, of the personality traits which we have called masculine or feminine are as lightly linked to sex as are the clothing, the manners, and the form of head-dress that a society at a given period assigns to either sex. ... The differences between individuals who are members of different cultures, like the differences between individuals within a culture, are almost entirely to be laid to differences in conditioning, especially during early childhood, and the form of this conditioning is culturally determined. Standardized personality differences between the sexes are of this order, cultural creations to which each generation, male and female, is trained to conform. There remains, however, the problem of the origin of these socially standardized differences.
>
> While the basic importance of social conditioning is still imperfectly recognized — not only in lay thought, but even by the scientist specifically concerned with such matters — to go beyond it and consider the possible influence of variations in hereditary equipment is a hazardous matter.

Third, the significance of woman's behavior and temperament depends upon the interpretation given them. Freud's theory that woman is filled with envy of man need not be interpreted as an indication of the effect of biological differences upon temperament. It might, instead, be seen as woman's reaction to her social status. Betty Friedan points out in *The Feminine Mystique*:

---

* Excerpted from Marjorie B. U'Ren, "The Image of Women in Textbooks" (Chap. 14), in *Woman in Sexist Society*, edited by Vivian Gornick and Barbara K. Moran. New York: Basic Books, Inc., © 1971.

If a woman was denied the freedom, the status and the pleasures that men enjoyed and wished secretly that she could have these things, in the shorthand of the dream, she might wish herself a man and see herself with the one thing which made men unequivocally different — the penis.

In the same way, other traditional feminine qualities such as woman's lack of aggression, emotionalism, and weakness of will may not be based upon biological differences at all but rather upon woman's needs as a social being.

Fourth, because woman is not yet treated as man's equal, any conclusions about the effect of biological differences upon temperament and behavior are biased. They are based upon social expectations of what woman ought to be rather than upon knowledge of what she is. Consequently, we do not and cannot know how biological differences affect the temperament and behavior of either man or woman. As Naomi Weisstein states, ". . . until social expectations for men and women are equal, until we provide equal respect for both men and women, our answers to this question will simply reflect our prejudices."

### VIEW: Woman Is Less Intelligent Than Man

The size of woman's brain has been considered a sign that woman is less intelligent than man since it was sometimes assumed that the larger the brain, the higher an animal's intelligence. But, in fact, this conclusion has been proven incorrect. As the anthropologist Ashley Montagu points out in *The Natural Superiority of Women*, scientific investigations have indicated that, ". . . *there is no relation whatever between brain size and intelligence.*" Ironically, as he also points out, ". . . in relation to total body size the female brain is at least as large as, and in general larger than, that of the male!"

Nevertheless, there is still a tendency to assume that woman is less intelligent and certainly less "clear-thinking" than man, concepts which continue to be reflected in our language. For example, it is considered a compliment to tell a woman that "she thinks like a man" or that she has a "masculine mind." A woman who disagrees with a man during an argument, on the other hand, may be told that she thinks "just like a woman."

The education of women in the United States suggests that woman may be less able to handle abstract thought than man is. As we saw in Chapter 2, women are likely to study a limited number of subjects, and few of these are subjects like mathematics, law, and philosophy, all of which are considered to require the ability to think abstractly.

Nevertheless, no one knows whether or not there are biological differences in intelligence or in the way each sex thinks. In his essay *On the Subjection of Women*, the nineteenth-century English philosopher John Stuart Mill argued that there are no differences at all, that ". . . any of the mental differences supposed to exist between women and men are but the natural effect of the differences in their education and circumstances. . . ."

Others, however, claim that there are genuine mental differences between the sexes, but that these are not differences in quality but rather in kind. That is, woman has a different type of intelligence than man, one which is more closely linked to her emotions. In *Preparing for Marriage*, Dr. John Marshall, for example, describes "a feminine outlook" as one ". . . with its tendency to a more intuitive, emotional, or downright illogical way of thinking." Dr. Montagu, on the other hand, praises the difference in woman's intelligence. He argues that woman is as intelligent as man but:

> The genius of woman is the genius of humanity, and humanity is the supreme form of intelligence. Mankind must learn to understand that all other forms of intelligence must be secondary to the developed *humane* intelligence, for any form of intelligence that is not primarily implanted into a matrix of humane feeling and understanding is the most dangerous thing in the world. The clever can never be too clever when they are governed by the desire and the ability to think of the welfare of others — even before they think of their own — for so to think and conduct oneself is to serve oneself better than one may in any other manner.
>
> It is that kind of intelligence that the world stands most in need of at the present time. It is that kind of intelligence that the world will always stand most in need of. It is that kind of intelligence with which women are so abundantly endowed. It is that kind of intelligence that it is their destiny to teach the world.

Those who, like John Stuart Mill, reject the view that woman is less intelligent than man or that she has a different type of intelligence than man respond with the following arguments.

There is no evidence that biological differences in intelligence between the sexes exist. As in the arguments opposing the concept of biological differences in temperament and behavior, they point out that any attempts to demonstrate these differences are invalid because they reflect the cultural biases of those involved. Furthermore, any differences in the way man and woman think can probably be explained more accurately as the result of cultural conditioning. Woman is taught to emphasize her emotions and is often discouraged from developing her mind. For example, a woman who is complimented because she thinks "like a man" is also being told at the same time that she is not exhibiting the feminine qualities society expects of her. In addition, the fields of study woman chooses are those which she is free to enter and which enable her to find employment. Rather than reflecting the quality of woman's mind, they reflect the conscious and unconscious limitations society imposes upon her.

Finally, they argue that until man and woman are treated as equals, our prejudices bar us from discovering what, if any, mental differences exist between the sexes. Therefore, it is preferable to assume that there are none and to offer woman the same opportunities man has to develop her intellectual potential.

### VIEW: Woman Is Less Creative Than Man

This view of woman is based upon a comparison of the contributions of man and woman to culture. Those who accept it argue correctly that there are no great women philosophers, composers, playwrights, or inventors. There are very few women who can be considered great painters, sculptors, novelists, poets, or scientists. We have, for example, no female Plato, Shakespeare, Da Vinci, or Einstein. The greatest thinkers and artists have always been men. Therefore, we might conclude that it is natural for woman to be less creative than man and that she has less to offer civilization.

To accept this view does not mean that we need think less of woman's accomplishments. In *Sex in Man and Woman*, Theodor Reik reports one woman's reaction to man's achievements.

We gladly admit that you men are more intelligent and accomplish many things in various fields. But we women have something more important to do. Without us mankind would be extinguished. We have to see to it that there are children in the world and that there are men and women in future generations.

Ashley Montagu argues that woman is not naturally less creative than man. If she wished to, she could achieve as much as he. She does not because:

> For the most part women are busy creatively living the life that men can only paint or write about. Because women live creatively, they rarely experience the need to depict or write about that which to them is a primary experience and which men know only at second remove. Women create naturally — men create artificially.

He points out, in addition, that woman actually has numerous achievements to her credit but that these are largely unrecognized.

> Her medium is humanity, and her materials are human beings. Her greatest works are unsigned, and fame and recognition are bestowed upon the work and not upon the artist.

Those who believe that woman's creative potential is equal to man's argue that woman has had fewer opportunities to realize it. In Western societies, for example, the education of woman on the same basis as man has developed slowly and primarily during the last century. As we have seen in Chapter 2, it is not yet complete. Before the idea of equal education for women became accepted, the majority of women did not have the chance to read or learn freely, and woman's education was largely limited to knowledge which would help her fulfill her duties as wife and mother.

In addition, most women are married and have little time or energy to devote to philosophy, science, or the arts. John Stuart Mill stated in *On the Subjection of Women*:

> There is, first, the superintendence of the family and the domestic expenditure, which occupies at least one woman in every family, generally the one of mature years and acquired experience; unless the family is so rich as to admit of delegating that task to hired agency, and submitting to all the waste and malversation inseparable from that mode of conducting it. The superintendence of a household, even when not in other respects laborious, is extremely onerous to the thoughts; it requires incessant vigilance, an eye which no detail escapes, and presents questions for consideration and solution, foreseen and unforeseen, at every hour of the

day, from which the person responsible for them can hardly ever shake herself free.

Therefore, what women achieve, if they achieve at all, is accomplished by stealing time for themselves. The modern poet Sylvia Plath, for instance, wrote early in the morning before her children awoke.

According to the novelist Virginia Woolf, in order for a woman to create she needs "five hundred pounds a year" and "a room of one's own." That is, she needs enough money to buy sufficient time for her work and a place where she is free to do it. Otherwise, she faces such overwhelming obstacles that she can never fulfill her potential.

Perhaps one of the most persuasive explanations for woman's lack of creative achievement is the fact that women have faced discrimination whenever they tried to enter fields open to men. For example, suppose that Shakespeare had had a sister who was equally gifted and who wanted a life in the theater? What might have happened to her? In *A Room of One's Own*, Virginia Woolf imagines her life, one which was very different from her brother's because she was a woman.

> She stood at the stage door; she wanted to act, she said. Men laughed in her face. The manager — a fat, loose-lipped man — guffawed. He bellowed something about poodles dancing and women acting—no woman, he said, could possibly be an actress. He hinted — you can imagine what. She could get no training in her craft. Could she even seek her dinner in a tavern or roam the streets at midnight? Yet her genius was for fiction and lusted to feed abundantly upon the lives of men and women and the study of their ways. At last — for she was very young, oddly like Shakespeare the poet in her face, with the same grey eyes and rounded brows — at last Nick Greene the actor-manager took pity on her; she found herself with child by that gentleman and so — who shall measure the heat and violence of the poet's heart when caught and tangled in a woman's body? — killed herself one winter's night and lies buried at some cross-roads where the omnibuses now stop outside the Elephant and Castle.

Even today, for those who believe in woman's creative potential, the story of "Shakespeare's sister" is fiction based firmly upon the truth of woman's experience.

## VIEW: Woman Is Inferior to Man and, Therefore, Should Be Dominated by Him

Belief in woman's inferiority is based upon the kinds of arguments we have been examining in our discussions of the sexual differences in behavior and temperament, intelligence, and creative achievement. If we accept these views and the arguments which support them, we are forced to conclude that woman is not capable of being man's equal, and that, as a result, she should acknowledge man's superiority and accept his domination.

This view has a long historical and social tradition, against which it is often difficult to argue. For example, most families are patriarchies, that is, according to *Webster's New World Dictionary*, groups ". . . in which the father or the eldest male is recognized as the head of the family or tribe, descent and kinship being traced through the male line." Responsibility for the care of the family is the husband's. He is "the breadwinner," who ultimately decides where *his* family should live and how. Frequently, he is in charge of disciplining the children, and deciding, therefore, the standards which they should live by.

The structure of so many societies, including our own, is patterned upon the patriarchal family that to conceive of another kind of structure requires an act of will and imagination. In most religions, for instance, God is assumed to be masculine, and the authorities of a church are usually male. Most governments, including our own, are headed and run by men, as are most other elements of society — from agriculture to commerce to entertainment. Everywhere we look we find that society is run by man and so affirms man's superiority.

As a result, it is not surprising to discover the view that woman should accept male domination. In his *Politics*, the Greek philosopher Aristotle assumed that it is natural for woman to be ruled by man.

> Of household management we have seen that there are three parts — one is the rule of a master over slaves, which has been discussed already, another of a father, and the third of a husband. A husband and father, we saw, rules over wife and children, both free, but the rule differs, the rule over his children being a royal, over his wife a constitutional rule. For although there may be exceptions to the order of

nature, the male is by nature fitter for command than the female, just as the elder and full-grown is superior to the younger and more immature.

In traditional Christian marriage services a similiar assumption is made when the bride agrees "to love, honor, and obey" her husband. What this implies is suggested by Shakespeare's Katherine, the tamed wife in *The Taming of the Shrew.*

Thy husband is thy lord, thy life, thy keeper,
Thy head, thy sovereign; one that cares for thee,
And for thy maintenance commits his body
To painful labour both by sea and land,
To watch the night in storms, the day in cold,
Whilst thou liest warm at home, secure and safe;
And craves no other tribute at thy hands
But love, fair looks, and true obedience —
Too little payment for so great a debt.
Such a duty as the subject owes the prince
Even such a woman oweth to her husband
And when she is froward, peevish, sullen, sour,
And not obedient to his honest will,
What is she but a foul contending rebel
And graceless traitor to her loving lord?

The view that woman should be dominated by man still is prevalent today. For example, it is reflected in our family structures and traditions, in most of the books we read in our schools, in the lower status of most women employees and in the fact that they usually work for a man, as well as in theories of social organization such as those presented by Professor Tiger, or theories of personality such as those presented by Sigmund Freud and his followers.

To summarize, the arguments in favor of woman's inferiority and subservience to man are supported by what we learn from history, sociology, psychology, religion, and literature and from our own observations of life around us.

Those who believe in full equal rights for woman reject these arguments and the evidence which supports them. They claim that woman's subservience to man is not the result of her innate inferiority. For example, in *Sexual Politics*, Kate Millett argues that it is instead the result of "politics," that is, ". . . power-structured relationships whereby one group of persons is controlled by another." The patriarchal pattern which most families, institutions, and societies follow has permitted man to dominate woman for his own benefit. Therefore, women represent an oppressed group which provides needed services such as house-keeping and child care without receiving adequate social or financial reward. In industrial societies like ours, they also per-form necessary but low-paying jobs and functions, according to Kate Millett, ". . . as a reserve labor force, enlisted in times of war and expansion and discharged in times of peace and reces-sion." Consequently, if we accept this argument, we can describe women as an exploited "minority" whose position is comparable to other minorities such as, for example, migrants, blacks, and Puerto Ricans. The only difference is that even within minorities women form a separate and lower group which continues to be oppressed and exploited.

Since one cannot exploit an equal, the concept of woman as inferior to man is used as a means of controlling her. Most of our cultural institutions and traditions — as exemplified in religion, social organization, psychology, and education — are used to justify woman's oppressed condition and to teach her to see her-self as the servant man expects her to be.

The result, according to John Stuart Mill in *On the Subjec-tion of Women*, is the creation of a society based upon injustice.

> All the selfish propensities, the self-worship, the unjust self-preference, which exist among mankind, have their source and root in, and derive their principal nourishment from, the present constitution of the relation between men and women.

In *The Second Sex*, the famous contemporary French writer Simone de Beauvoir also argues that woman's oppression is a destructive social force.

> The woman who is shut up in immanence endeavors to hold man in that prison also; thus the prison will be con-fused with the world, and woman will no longer suffer from being confined there: mother, wife, sweetheart are the jailers. Society, being codified by man, decrees that woman is inferior: she can do away with this inferiority only by destroying the male's superiority. She sets about mutilating, dominating man, she contradicts him, she denies his truth and his values. But in doing this she is only defending her-

self; it was neither a changeless essence nor a mistaken choice that doomed her to immanence, to inferiority. They were imposed upon her. All oppression creates a state of war. And this is no exception. The existent who is regarded as inessential cannot fail to demand the re-establishment of her sovereignty.

The question of how to achieve equality, however, is difficult to answer. Modern societies which have tried to bring about sexual equality have not succeeded completely. For example, one aim of the Russian revolution was equal rights for women, and liberal divorce and abortion laws were passed soon after the revolution was won. But these were later replaced by less liberal ones, and today few Russian women hold positions of power. The Israel kibbutz began as a revolutionary movement in which equal rights for women was a major goal. Yet after his visit to Israel during 1964, the psychiatrist Bruno Bettelheim reported in *The Children of the Dream* that, "Women have more and more been assigned to the work tasks considered 'feminine,' such as child rearing, kitchen and laundry, etc."

To believe in equal rights for women, then, does not mean that they will be realized. For the creation of a society in which man and woman are truly equal requires a sharp break with our cultural traditions and habits, and an uncharted journey into the unknown.

## VIEW: The Proper Roles for Woman Are Wife and Mother

This view evolves naturally from woman's biological functions. Woman alone bears children and, particularly in primitive societies, feeds them during the first months of life. Therefore, we can say, that the survival of the human race depends upon woman. The assumption that one of woman's primary roles is child care simply extends woman's biological functions beyond the periods of her pregnancy and a child's infancy.

Being a wife is related to woman's role as mother. As we have discussed earlier, most families are patriarchal. Usually in such families labor is shared by the parents. The father's function is to provide shelter, food, and clothing for his wife and children. The mother's is to care for the household and the children. In other words, a wife performs those tasks which free her husband to fulfill his responsibilities as provider.

How marriage and woman's role in the family were first established is not known. Sigmund Freud argued in *Civilization and Its Discontents* that marriage and the concept of the family originated when men decided upon a permanent sexual partner. Woman, ". . . who did not want to be separated from her helpless young, was obliged, in their interests, to remain with the stronger male." According to Freud, then, woman was willing to become a wife because she was a mother.

Some believe, however, that marriage is a feminine creation. In *The Liberated Woman and Other Americans*, Midge Decter writes, " . . . marriage and children are not things imposed on women by men but quite the other way around." Marriage " . . . is not a psychic relationship but a transaction: in which a man foregoes the operations of his blind boyhood lust, and agrees to undertake the support and protection of a family, and receives in exchange the ease and comforts of home."

Being wife and mother are often thought of as woman's natural roles, those which best fulfill her physical and psycho-logical needs. For example, in *Sex in Man and Woman*, Theodor Reik states:

> Women mold themselves and identify themselves more readily with their love-objects [than do men]. They might admire individuality in men, but they do not like the alone-ness and loneliness connected with it. They will never agree with Ibsen's saying that the strong ones are more powerful when alone. They are much more sociable than men. Nature has prepared them for their future role of wife and mother much more than she has men for their part as husbands and fathers which is rather a role men have to improvise when they become head of a family.

He concluded that in order for a woman to be " . . . a valuable and useful member of society . . . ," she " . . . should, in the ideal case, fulfill three requirements: she should be a good wife, a good mother, and a good mistress. It is, however, enough to fulfill two of these three demands."

Ashley Montagu agrees with Reik's view of woman's role, but he stresses the importance of motherhood.

> The most important of women's tasks is the making of human beings in cooperation with their husbands. In this happiest and most rewarding of all labors of love, women

bear a great responsibility, for they hold not less than the future in their hands.

Anthony Storr argues that because of woman's roles as wife and mother:

> Women have no need to compete with men; for what they alone can do is the more essential. Love, the bearing of children and the making of a home are creative activities without which we should perish. . . .

From the point of view of those involved in the women's rights movement, however, the limitation of woman's role to wife and mother symbolizes woman's oppressed state. They argue that often woman performs these labors without love, that they hinder her from achieving equality with man, and that they offer her little reward.

In particular, they attack the notion that housework is in any way equal in prestige or personal satisfaction to the work man does. They consider it a service which woman renders man at her own personal expense, in exchange for clothing, food, and shelter, so that man is free to pursue his interests. They claim that the repetition of a housewife's chores — the constant cleaning, shopping, cooking — dulls woman's mind and makes her feel, as Betty Freidan writes in *The Feminine Mystique*, "trapped, frustrated, guilty." Woman's attitude toward housework, therefore, is, according to Betty Freidan, " . . . a clear signal that *women have outgrown the housewife role.*"

Whether or not woman is satisfied with her role as housewife, the chores remain to be done, and they are necessary for the welfare of the family. In addition, both tradition and law claim that they are the wife's responsibility. Therefore, suggestions by those in the women's rights movement to change woman's role as housewife have serious implications for marriage and the traditional roles assigned to each sex.

Some suggest that caring for a home is less important than doing work one enjoys. In addition, they argue, the idea of a "spic and span" house is out-of-date. Others argue that marriage should become more equalitarian, with all chores shared by husband and wife, since both live in the home. During an interview with Sandra Lipsitz and Daryl Bem, printed in *MS.* Magazine, May 1972, Claude Servan-Schreiber records the way one married couple handles household chores.

SANDY: Things that have to be done every day get routinized. Cooking, for example, and cleaning up. For this we alternate every other night.

Still others argue for a more revolutionary solution. In her article "Slavery or Labor of Love," printed in "Notes from the Third Year: Women's Liberation," Betsy Warrior recommends:

> ... the abolition of "housework" and "domestic" service in the sense that it is now known. Once this work has to be paid for, it will be incorporated into the "public" economy. This means that the work that was formerly done in separate, duplicated single units will be collectivized and industrialized on a large basis with a more efficient use of both time and labor and without the waste, alienation, and duplication now involved in child care and home maintenance. Only when this is accomplished will women be able to fight for their equality on a more nearly equal footing with men.

If these solutions, or others like them, become accepted by large numbers of families, they will alter the traditional concept of marriage and the definition of a wife.

Woman's traditional role as mother has also been questioned by those in the women's rights movement. They argue that child care is but another example of woman's oppression. A mother is expected to sacrifice herself for her children, to place their interests over her own, just as a wife is expected to do the same for her husband. Consequently, the responsibilities of motherhood hinder woman from achieving her own potential as a human being. The results are destructive to woman, man, and child. For instance, a mother who is frustrated and unhappy with her role may communicate her dissatisfactions to her children. She may, in addition, in order to live at all, try to "live" through her children, thus placing a heavy emotional burden upon them. She may even try to dominate or dehumanize her children in order to achieve a sense of power.

Those who reject woman's traditional role in child care argue that children would benefit if their mothers were fulfilled human beings. Betty Freidan suggests in *The Feminine Mystique*:

> We have gone on too long blaming or pitying the mothers who devour their children, who sow the seeds of progressive

dehumanization, because they have never grown to full humanity themselves. If the mother is at fault, why isn't it time to break the pattern by urging all these Sleeping Beauties to grow up and live their own lives?

They argue that bringing up children should not be considered a full-time job, that woman should spend much of her time in activities which satisfy her needs.

Furthermore, they argue that the conditions of modern society, particularly in the United States, are harmful for raising children. Too many families live in small, isolated dwellings, with the family consisting of father, mother, and children. Usually, the father works outside the home. Because he is away for most of the day, he may become a stranger to his children, seeing them only briefly in the evenings and on weekends. Lacking time, he frequently has little responsibility in his children's upbringing. The mother, on the other hand, is trapped in the house, often with young children as her constant companions, and she may rarely see other adults for most of the day. She has, therefore, too much time and attention to devote to her children. Consequently, children — especially young children — are very limited in their social contacts with adults, their mother often being the only one they know well. One argument for the development of numerous group child care centers derives from the type of family situation we have described. It is argued that through these centers young children would have increased social contact with adults and that, as a result, they would have a greater variety of models of adult behavior upon which to pattern themselves.

In conclusion, those who reject the view that woman's proper roles are wife and mother argue that the limitations of woman's functions in this way ultimately diminish human beings and harm society. These traditional roles, they argue, can no longer be justified as we move into the twenty-first century. They create unhappy, dissatisfied, and angry women who resent their husbands and children and who, as a result, often hinder them from achieving their potential. Consequently, this view of woman contributes to the growth of a society which is increasingly dehumanized. Unless sexual roles disappear and sexual equality is realized, there is no hope for more humane relationships between people or for a more humane world.

## Further Readings

The following works are recommended for further study of the topics discussed in this chapter.

1. de Beauvoir, Simone. *The Second Sex.* Translated by H. M. Parshley. New York: Knopf, 1953. (Also a Bantam paperback; a scholarly study of woman's status in society by a major contemporary French writer.)

2. Freidan, Betty. *The Feminine Mystique.* New York: Norton, 1963. (Also a Dell paperback; one of the first and major works about contemporary woman's position in the United States, written by the founder of the National Organization for Women.)

3. Freud, Sigmund. "Femininity," *New Introductory Lectures on Psychoanalysis.* Translated and edited by James Strachey. New York: Norton, 1965. (Also a Norton paperback; a study of the effect of biological differences upon woman's temperament and behavior by the founder of psychoanalysis.)

4. Figes, Eva. *Patriarchal Attitudes.* New York: Stein & Day, 1970. (Also a Fawcett paperback; a study of sexual bias in culture and its effect upon women.)

5. Gornick, Vivian, and Moran, Barbara K., eds. *Woman in Sexist Society.* New York: Basic Books, 1971. (Also a Signet paperback; an anthology of essays written by feminists which cover a variety of topics about the contemporary status of women.)

6. Greer, Germaine. *The Female Eunuch.* New York: McGraw-Hill, 1971. (Also a Bantam paperback; a study of the effect of sexual inequality upon women by a feminist.)

7. Ibsen, Henrik. *A Doll's House, Ghosts and Three Other Plays.* Translated by Michael Meyer. Garden City, New York: Doubleday, 1966. (An Anchor paperback; a late nineteenth-century play which deals with the problems of woman's rights and role in marriage, written by the great modern Norwegian playwright.)

8. Kanowitz, Leo. *Women and the Law: The Unfinished Revolution.* Albuquerque, New Mexico: University of New Mexico Press, 1969. (Also a paperback; a study of legal discrimination against women.)

9. Mailer, Norman. *The Prisoner of Sex.* Boston: Little, Brown, 1971. (Also a Signet paperback; a well-known American novelist responds to the issues raised by the women's rights movement.)

10. Mead, Margaret. *Sex and Temperament in Three Primitive*

*Societies.* New York: William Morrow, 1935. (Also a Dell paperback; a study of sexual differences in temperament and the effect of social conditioning by a famous contemporary anthropologist.)

11. Mill, John Stuart. *On the Subjection of Women.* Introduction by Susan Brownmiller. Greenwich, Conn.: Fawcett, 1971. (A Fawcett Premier paperback; an essay which argues in favor of women's rights and sexual equality by the great nineteenth century English philosopher.)

12. Millett, Kate. *Sexual Politics.* Garden City, New York: Doubleday, 1970. (Also a paperback; a study of the political aspects of sexual inequality and an examination of sexual politics in four writers.)

13. Montagu, Ashley. *The Natural Superiority of Women.* rev. ed. New York: Macmillan, 1968. (Also a Collier paperback; a famous anthropologist's views about the belief in male supremacy and woman's roles.)

14. Morgan, Robin, ed. *Sisterhood Is Powerful.* New York: Random House, 1970. (Also a paperback; a collection of writings from the women's liberation movement.)

15. *MS.* Magazine. (A monthly feminist magazine which carries numerous articles of interest.)

16. Reik, Theodor. *Sex in Man and Woman: Its Emotional Variations.* New York: Farrar, Straus & Giroux, 1960. (Also a Bantam paperback; the conclusions of a famous psychiatrist about the effect of sexual differences upon behavior and temperament.)

17. Schneir, Miriam, ed. *Feminism: The Essential Historical Writings.* New York: Random House, 1972. (A Vintage paperback; a collection of excerpts from the writings of major feminists.)

18. Storr, David. *Human Aggression.* New York: Atheneum, 1968. (Also a Bantam paperback; a discussion by an English psychiatrist of aggression in man's behavior.)

19. *The Black Scholar,* December, 1971. (An issue devoted completely to the black woman.)

20. Tiger, Lionel. *Men in Groups.* New York: Random House, 1969. (Also a Vintage paperback; a study of male grouping and its relationship to biology which supports the theory of innate sexual differences.)

21. Women's Bureau, United States Department of Labor. *Handbook on Women Workers.* Washington, D. C.: Government Print-

ing Office, published periodically. (A valuable source of factual information on such matters as women's work, salary, and education as well as the laws which affect women.)

22. Woolf, Virginia. *A Room of One's Own*. New York: Harcourt, Brace & World, 1929. (Also a Harbinger paperback; an essay, written by a major modern English novelist, about women and fiction which discusses the effect of sexual inequality upon woman's creativity.)

# Chapter 5

# Equality in 2001

There is no doubt that the status of women in the United States will change in the future. The movement for women's rights is so large and so active that it must influence the way our country grows. Therefore, the major question is: What will life be like for our children?

The following stories offer two very different answers. Both are extreme examples of what could occur. As you read them, try to decide which seems to suggest the direction the United States will take and what might really happen.

### Pages from a Notebook Found in San Diego

I've been here for only two weeks, but it seems longer. I was a fool to come, I suppose. Perhaps I should have argued, although I'm not certain — it might have been dangerous. Once the Committee makes a decision, you have no choice really. And they were suspicious of me, I know it.

"You need a rest, Gloria," the Director said. "You're tired and nervous. The doctor at the camp thinks that you're on the verge of a serious depression. You've been at your station for almost a year now — a long time to face the enemy."

I was convinced. It seemed such a good idea, to be able to sleep again, to rest, to walk along the beach far from the front, where there would be no chance of an enemy attack. Peaceful. I wanted peace.

I hadn't slept well for months. I kept wondering about the enemy, kept seeing him.

93

The sleeping cure hasn't helped at all. I thought it would when I asked for it. Five days of drugged sleep! It was as though I had died, only I knew it, I knew I was suspended in space and time, lost somewhere in the world of the dead. Since the treatment, I've felt even more depressed. I feel as though I've lost all control over myself. And I'm so tired, so tired of everything.

I kept seeing his face while I was sleeping. I didn't tell the doctor, of course. They don't realize you can dream even when you're taking the cure, that the dreams are the same or worse than being awake. That must be why I'm so tired — from dreaming, from seeing his face, and trying to touch him, to bring him back.

It's ironic, really. They've controlled so much of us and yet they can't control the dreams, at least, not yet. They will in time, just like everything else.

I keep seeing his face — that boy I killed. He was so young. He looked 15, although I suppose he was older. I'm not sure what the minimum age is in their army, but it must be the same as ours. Children can't be soldiers. Yes, he must have been older, that makes sense. If he hadn't looked so young, I know I wouldn't feel this way.

And I didn't realize that he wasn't carrying a gun until after I'd shot him. I didn't think about it at all. What fool would be wandering on the enemy side of the border without a gun? He must have been on a reconnaissance mission, he must have! Why else would he cross the river? He shouldn't have come. He was too young, too inexperienced! Didn't he realize that we'd kill him?

He looked so surprised when he saw me, as though he had seen a strange animal. Even after he was dead, he still looked surprised — unsure of what had happened or why.

I suppose I was the first woman he'd ever seen. And it must have shocked him, to be walking in the woods and suddenly come face to face with a woman. Did he wonder what we are like?

I know when I was at school, I used to be curious about man, what kind of a beast he was — with hair covering most of his body, even growing on his face. The zoologists are right, of course. Hair like that is the sign of a primitive animal. It serves no purpose unless as a beast man needs it for body covering. Yes, man must be a lower animal, not quite fully human, but an earlier evolutionary stage in the development of woman.

His muscular body, for example, is another clear sign. In this day and age, when machines can do all the heavy work, of what use are muscles?

Still, the boy looked so weak. Poor thing, lying there, blood trickling down his cheek. I touched the wound and felt the blood. It was warm. Lying there, dead, he seemed so gentle that he looked like a young girl.

I would have liked to talk to him, to have found out what it is like on his side. We really don't know very much about the enemy's country. Do they live in groups as we do? Do they have Committees to watch over them, to make sure they are taken care of? What was the effect of the war on them?

Yes, I wish I had talked to him. I wish I had taken the chance to know what a man is like.

My mother remembered when men and women lived together, before the war. She had a father. My mother told me no one knew in those days what kind of child would be born. If a family was lucky, it was a girl. But it might be a boy, or, even worse, a child who was deformed.

My birth was better. At least by then we had artificial insemination and mother knew what the child she carried would be. But things are even better now, since the child development centers were built. They are a major improvement, and more humane, too. A woman doesn't have to use her strength to carry a child in her womb.

We can make certain now that the children are superior — girls, with perfect minds and bodies. It makes more sense than the old way. The health of the child isn't dependent upon a mother. And the nurses can watch the fetus in the incubator, make sure that it is growing normally, and if it isn't destroy it. There's no throwback either, no chance with our controls of giving birth to a boy or a deformed child.

I suppose I might have felt differently if I had lived before the war. But that was such a different world that I can barely imagine it.

Mother said grandmother used to talk about it. "A man's world," she called it, a world in which women were treated like slaves, with no rights that mattered. They could vote for a man but not for a woman. Women didn't have any power at all.

I suppose the war was inevitable. How long could women go on as they were, denying their own psychological needs, keeping themselves from improving the species?

I wonder what lies that boy learned about us in school. What was he told about the revolution? Does the enemy celebrate February 5 as we do? Do they have their own day of liberation?

I wish I could get his face out of my mind. If I told a psychiatrist she'd probably help me. But I'm afraid. Suppose she felt that I was becoming a deviant, a danger to the community? No, it's better to write it out for myself, to think it through on paper. Then I'll cure myself and no one will know.

The Committee wouldn't want to know. They'd have to investigate me, and that might be embarrassing for them. After all, I am the granddaughter of a hero of the revolution.

What would they do to me? Another sleep cure, perhaps. I don't think I could live through that — the dreams, the lack of control, the awakening, and the horrible memory of being drugged. They say lots of women commit suicide after a sleep cure.

They'd try something, of course. They wouldn't want to put me in the Rehabilitation Center, at least not at first. After all, my grandmother helped create the revolution. She was one of the first women of the new era.

I wish I had known her. She must have been a remarkable human being. Left alone at twenty-five, deserted by her husband. He'd just walked out of the house, leaving her with a six-month old baby and ten dollars! Ten dollars! My mother told me he must have hated his family to desert them in a strange city with no money. They might have starved, I suppose, if my grandmother had been a weaker woman. But she had courage, real courage.

She got herself a job cleaning offices at night. It was the best she could do, a woman without a high school education, with no friends or money, and a small daughter to care for. She'd take mother with her and watch her while she cleaned.

It must have been a lonely life, coming late at night to a building which was almost completely empty, working without seeing anyone. It must have been hard, too, sweeping, dusting, emptying the trash. She probably aged quickly. I suppose she became angrier as she worked, cleaning the offices of rich men and thinking of how her husband had treated her. More than most women, my grandmother must have understood that the revolution was necessary.

I wonder how she first became involved in the Revolutionary Committee. Who brought her to that first meeting? I guess no one knows. At least the history books never mention it. Even the Committee's official biography doesn't discuss it.

To think she worked secretly for more than ten years, cleaning at night, and planning with the Committee the first tentative battles. I suppose no one expected the revolution to turn out as it did — with the continent cut in two.

Originally the goal was equality, with men and women living together. When the movement began, no one dreamed that was an impossible goal.

If men had been more reasonable the war could have been avoided. Of course, to expect rationality in men is unreasonable itself, a sign of illogical masculine thinking. The Committee, though, must have first thought of the possibility. Why else would they have wasted so much time attacking laws, trying to achieve equality through the courts and the government? They should have known better.

But I suppose all those years of male domination must have taken their toll. It must have meant that they needed to shake off the old habits of the mind, to learn to think like women.

When the struggle failed, they had to turn to the alternative of war. They had no other choice. Now that they knew men were the enemy, they had to be more careful, to stockpile weapons, to plan their actions without arousing suspicion.

The most difficult problem, though, at least in the early days, must have been recruitment. It must have been hard to meet secretly with other women, to try to convince them that their fathers, husbands, and sons *were* the enemy, that they had no choice but to take up arms against them.

And the numerous meetings in the homes of the Committee, the long tedious days building the weapons they needed. Working secretly, with little hope, but with a vision of freedom must have taken almost all their strength! Since there had never been a revolution like this before in the history of the world, they were working out their own destiny in darkness, shaking off centuries of servitude without any assurance that they could win.

But they did win, they did win!

After that bloody war, which killed more than half the male population, we'd won. February 5! Oh, how I wish I could have been there, following my grandmother into the White House, sitting with her at the conference table. What pleasure it must have given her to see the defeated enemy standing before her! What joy to watch the President of the United States take up his pen and sign the treaty, dividing the country in half, agreeing that all land west of the Mississippi was to be woman's new home, inviolate, hers forever! What delight she must have felt as she walked away from the table, knowing the days of servitude for all women were over forever! Oh, to have been alive then, to have been one of the soldiers in the revolution!

Why, then, does the death of one boy depress me? Why do I keep seeing his face, looking so surprised and so young? Why can't I be like the others — a good soldier — eager to kill for my country? What's the matter with me?

Maybe it's my inheritance, the blood of my grandfather running through me. Oh, I wish I had been born in the incubator like the new children! But I'm an anachronism, developed in a woman's womb, the last generation to have a mother, to be able to trace its lines back in history to the years before the revolution. Once my generation is gone, there will be no more impurities, no inheritances of blood to fear.

No woman born today would feel as I do about that boy. She'd know that "to pity the enemy is to destroy woman's freedom."

But I wish, I wish, I wish — *I had not killed him.*

I wish he and I had talked. I'd never had the chance to speak to a man before. I felt I could talk to him, that we could understand each other. He looked so much like a girl that I think we might even have become friends.

There's so much I'd like to know about life over there. Is it like ours? What do they eat? Do they dance? What do they learn about us? Lies, I suppose, lies. That's to be expected. Perhaps we've been taught lies, too.

Oh, no, you mustn't think that! It's treason and you know it isn't true. Women don't lie.

But why do we continue to hate men so much? After all these years, why are we still raised on hate, our minds filled with stories of the atrocities women suffered? We live in hate, as though we need it to give us the energy to survive.

But it has to stop sometime. We can't continue this way, justifying everything we do by our hatred of men. We harm ourselves. We need to spend our time building our own society, not thinking of destroying theirs.

And we need the men. They are our neighbors. Someday we must begin again to know them. No country can remain isolated, turned in on itself. After all, we share the same continent. Someday we must put down our guns and begin to talk, to trade with each other.

Of course, the continent will never be united again. I'm sure of that. It's too late for men and women to live together in our society. But we should be able to live in peace with one another.

\*     \*     \*

I must destroy this notebook. If someone finds it, I will be in danger. I'm sure I'd be brought up before the Committee. This time, if they found the notebook, they wouldn't send me to a rest home. This time it would be the Rehabilitation Center. I know it!

I must be careful.

. . . I must not write anymore.

. . . I must be careful what I say.

. . . I must watch what I think.

. . . Spies are everywhere.

### A Letter from Santa Fe

Dear Edith,

We've been here six months now, and I feel settled at last. I can't tell you how pleased Harold and I are with it.

Taking time to choose was the right decision after all. For a while, I thought we were crazy to spend almost a year wandering around the country, trying to find *the* commune for us. I suppose we looked rather foolish. But being New Yorkers, neither of us felt sure where we wanted to be. All we knew was that we wanted to leave the crowded Northeast, to try someplace new.

I must say the Housing Office was most sympathetic to our plan. They arranged the whole itinerary, even suggesting particular places they thought we'd like. By the way, they now have complete records on all communes — including age groups, number of children, types of housing, jobs available, and special interests of those living there.

Harold definitely wanted to continue teaching. He loves, really loves, working with young children. And he's good with them, too, gentle, kind, and very imaginative. It was less difficult to place him because there seems to be a need again for teachers. I caused a good deal more trouble, however. I had decided, definitely, to try farming. I suppose that's the result of growing up in a city! The problem was for us to find a place we liked where I could work and study. My interest in farming developed so late that I was afraid that the government would try to discourage me from taking it up, particularly since it was clear that I didn't know a thing about it.

All turned out well, though. The Housing Office recommended a dozen communes in the South and the West and made arrangements for us to visit each for at least a month.

For a while, it looked as though we'd settle outside Durham, North Carolina. Both of us liked the area — green and lush, with rolling hills. The commune was a new one, started about five years ago by ten couples, all in their 20s and all from Massachusetts.

There are now about 30 families in the group, and it is still growing. They want a total of 50 families so that they can diversify more. At this point, they are primarily involved in truck farming, but they want to begin a pottery center as soon as they can. Evidently, at one time, North Carolina was famous for its pottery, and I think the group plans to revive the traditions in that area.

They were a friendly bunch and extremely energetic. They all live in three enormous old houses which they are in the process of restoring. They've also built a new community center, which houses a meeting room, kitchen, dining room, theater, and library. Since everyone eats there, they all meet several times a day and, as a result, they are very close.

Cooperation is good. Jobs are assigned on a monthly basis. Everyone does everything. One month, for example, you might work on the farm, the next develop future plans for the group, the third, work in the community center, etc.

We liked them very much. Almost everyone was our age and, as I said before, from our part of the country, so we had a good deal in common. We enjoyed ourselves so much that we stayed almost three months.

In the end, though, Harold and I decided not to join. Both of us wanted to be able to devote all of our time to our work. Although I liked the diversity, I found it tiring — there were just too many changes for me. Also, I would have had to study at Chapel Hill, rather a long way from the commune, and the offerings in agriculture were not very exciting.

As we moved West, we tried a few other places, but none seemed just right for us. The group in St. Louis, for example, lived in apartment complexes, the kind of old suburban developments which were built in the seventies and which, unfortunately, are still too common around New York. Neither of us could stand to live in them! Although the people were nice enough, the group in Oklahoma was just not compatible. I was beginning to wonder whether we should have stayed in North Carolina after all. At least there we felt at home.

But a few weeks later we came here, and I think we knew at once that this was the right place for us.

First of all, the area around Santa Fe is the most beautiful I've ever seen. There is a sense of space — miles and miles of open land, lots of it almost desert. Some of it is beginning to be reclaimed, by irrigation, so that here and there are a few patches of small green forests or fields of wheat. The mesas — low, flat hills — are startling, particularly at twilight, when they turn a deep rich purple.

Our commune is one of the oldest in the country. It was started in the late 1960s by a group of 20 students who had come out from the East. Now there are about 500 adults living here so that except for replacing those few who leave, it is full.

It has great variety. Like the group in North Carolina, there is a community building which houses the dining room, kitchen, meeting hall, library, art rooms, and entertainment centers. Living arrangements, however, are more various.

There are five dormitories which hold ten people each. Anyone who wants to can live there in a truly communal fashion. The dormitories are usually filled with a combination of couples and singles. Each dormitory has, in addition, two one-bed cabins nearby, so that those who want to be alone for a night or so can find privacy.

The rest of the community live in small one- and two-room houses. Many of these were built in the seventies, when the commune was first growing, but they've been kept in good shape. Harold and I chose to live in one of the houses, at least for the first six months or year.

Every six months, people are free to change their residences, if they wish to. Frank and Melba, two of our friends, moved last week from a house into a dormitory, just for "the change."

There are so many good things about life here that I don't really know where to begin. I like the fact that all ages and races live here together. One of the aims of the commune is human diversity (they believe it is healthier for the community) so they often look for replacements that other communes might not want — singles and elderly people, for example. As a result, there is no feeling, as I think there was in the North Carolina group, that everyone is the same.

I also like the belief in community ownership of goods.

Nothing is owned privately except our clothes, and even these are provided by the commune. So quite often we exchange or "lend" our clothes to others.

We choose our own work. Harold is teaching ten children, ages five to nine. Schools here are ungraded and quite often the age range is even greater than in the group he has. Since students progress as fast as they wish, the teacher can work with any age, and much of what he does is individual. Harold is very, very happy. He takes the children on picnics, wanders in and out of the community house and into the fields — all to teach the students by observation what they want to know.

Children, by the way, stay in school and at the commune only until the age of 15. After that, they are free to remain or, if they prefer, to travel for a year (at our expense!), or to leave the commune altogether. If they want to leave, we help them find another place. About half of the 15 year olds travel and then choose to return. The rest settle elsewhere.

Oh, I must tell you that children begin to live in their own dormitories when they are six weeks old. The community has been doing this almost since its founding. The members feel that after six weeks a child no longer needs intimate parental care, and that it is better for both the parents and the child to take him out of the house. Immediately after birth, however, both parents devote themselves full-time to caring for the new-born infant so that he can receive all the attention he needs without fatiguing one parent too much. At six weeks, however, the child is placed in the infant dormitory and both parents return to their jobs.

Although the children know their parents and sometimes spend a good deal of time with them, the belief here is that all adults are part of a child's family, that a child is everyone's responsibility and pleasure. It's not uncommon for one of the single men or women to become so attached to several children that they speak of them as their own.

The children are cared for with great love. Once a year each of us spends a month living in the infant dormitory so we come to know the new children very well. We're assigned in groups of four — two men and two women — but couples are assigned only if they request to work in the dormitory together. The community has found that often it is inconvenient for both to leave their jobs at the same time.

Then, once a year, for another month, two men and two women are assigned to sleep in a dormitory which houses children under six. Usually, couples take this assignment together since it doesn't interfere with one's job. Children at that age are really great fun — Harold and I thoroughly enjoyed our assignment with them!

After the age of six, the children sleep alone, without any adults around. The community believes that by six, children are old enough to care for themselves and for each other. If someone gets sick, for example, one of the children simply calls the doctor.

During the day, children under five are handled by specially trained teachers, who volunteer for their jobs as we all do. There is one group for children under a year, another for children one to three years old, and a third for children three to five. Since child care requires a very long day — from 7:00 A.M. to 8:00 P.M. — the teachers work in one of two shifts (morning or afternoon). Because of the nature of their jobs, they are exempt from working in the weekly clean-up crews. For the few hours they have kitchen duties, they are replaced by volunteers who want a chance to play with the children. There is one teacher for every five children so no child can possibly be neglected.

The commune tries to balance the sexes so that for each group half the teachers are men and half women. Although this kind of work doesn't interest me very much, I'm told that it is very popular. Consequently, there are more than enough qualified people who are willing to work at another job temporarily until an opening appears.

All routine jobs are shared. We work a four-day week here for the most part, although, of course, the hours vary according to the job. About five hours a week are spent in cleaning crews. During this time, groups clean the community house, the individual houses, and the dormitories.

Cooking, which as you know is not my favorite activity, is also shared. Twenty of us are assigned for three weeks to one meal. We divide the chores — some of us shop, others cook, and still others serve and clean up. For the most part, we volunteer for the jobs we prefer. We all spend only about two months a year in the kitchen, thank goodness. I've already worked the dinner shift. I had dreaded it, but, as it turned out, it was rather pleasant. Harold and I were assigned together, and our group was a good one — efficient, cooperative, and fun to work with. Being together made it seem less of a chore to me.

In general, I think "efficient, cooperative, and fun" sums up my feelings about the community. Some of this arises, I suppose, because no one has to stay. Each year we sign on for another, although actually most people remain permanently.

Also, the running of the community is shared by all of us. Once a year a management board is elected. Since the commune began in those days when women were still fighting for their rights, the tradition of conscious equality exists. The board, which is made up of 14 members, has to be composed of seven men and seven women, half of whom have never served before. The board handles the day-to-day routines. Any suggestions for change are brought to the board which then presents them to the entire community at the monthly meeting. If a suggestion is voted down but is one which does not affect the normal routine of the community, it can still be realized, usually on a more limited basis. For example, at the first meeting I attended, one man wanted to begin a weaving factory so that the commune could make and sell rugs. The motion was received with very little enthusiasm. But the community agreed to buy two looms so that the few people who were interested could try them out, and money was given them to visit some factories in California.

Of course, things don't always go smoothly. People living together are bound to disagree sometimes or to fight with one another. The weekly "gripe" sessions, however, where we talk about our irritations, go a long way toward ending them. Also, I think most of us here feel that the commune is such a good place to be that we want to protect it by working together. Most of the time we are doing exactly what we want to do, and we share all the work which because it becomes tedious might turn us into petty or envious people.

I suppose the main reason I love it here is my job. Farming is an important activity since the commune began as a way of returning to the land. We grow our own food, of course, but the major crop is wheat. A good deal of land is being reclaimed by irrigation, and there is continual experimentation to increase the yield or to develop new strains.

Everyone has been very patient with me, accepting my ignorance and teaching me what I need to know. For the last two months, I've been working with Jane, who is developing a hybrid which can withstand the sudden frosts and dry spells we get here. She hopes eventually to develop one which — far-fetched as it sounds — could grow even in the winter snows.

It was lucky for me and my work that we decided upon this commune. When we first came here, I didn't realize that it is considered one of the best wheat farms in the country and that Jane, who is a quiet, unassuming person, has a national reputation! As a result, I couldn't have a better place in which to work.

I'm also taking two courses at the Agricultural Center in Santa Fe, which is only a few miles away. Again, I was lucky. Because reclaiming the land is an important issue in New Mexico, the school is excellent. I had no problems being admitted either, and I can choose the courses I need.

As you probably realize by now I am really very, very happy with my life. Both Harold and I feel pleased with ourselves because we are doing exactly what we want. I'm so glad that neither of us had to sacrifice himself for the other, that we found a place where both of us are free to follow our interests.

Recently we've been talking about having a child. Harold would like to have one soon, but I'm less certain. I want to learn more. Even though a pregnant woman can work as long as she wishes, I don't feel like giving up six weeks, as we must do once the child is born. I'd rather wait another year or so. Harold says, "It's your decision," which means that at this point our child is a being of the future!

By the way, I may visit New York for a few days in late August. All members of the community receive a six-week vacation, and we are taking ours in July and August.

Harold wants to go to Japan to study the ancient Noh theater. I'm not anxious to join him since there are some farming centers I want to visit. It looks as though we'll take separate vacations this year since our interests aren't the same.

I plan to go to Texas first, then begin moving East, ending up in Northern Virginia. New York is less than two hours away by monorail, so I thought I'd come up for a visit. Are you free?

Write soon.

All my best,<br>Helen

# Chapter 6

# To Continue . . .

This book provides only a general introduction to the vast subject of women's rights. You may wish now to (1) add to your knowledge by studying the subject in greater depth; and/or (2) become involved in improving women's status.

The activities listed in this chapter suggest ways of doing both. They include topics you can study to increase your knowledge and actions you can take to bring about social change.

## I. Independent Study

The following topics are recommended for further study.

A. *The history of feminism*

1. the growth of feminism in the United States
2. the growth of feminism in Europe
3. the growth of feminism in Socialist or Communist countries

B. *Important feminists and their works*

1. Mary Wollstonecraft
2. Elizabeth Stanton
3. Sojourner Truth
4. Susan B. Anthony
5. Margaret Fuller
6. Margaret Sanger

7.   Betty Freidan
8.   Kate Millett

C. *The history of women workers in the United States*

1.   the employment of women before the Industrial Revolution
2.   the employment of women after the Industrial Revolution
3.   women's struggle for improved working conditions
4.   women's role in the development of labor unions
5.   women's role today in labor unions

D. *Women's legal status*

1.   women's status in colonial America
2.   women's status before 1920
3.   changes in women's status from 1920 to the present
4.   a comparison of women's status in eastern and western states

E. *Famous women in history*

1.   Queen Elizabeth I of England
2.   Mary, Queen of Scots
3.   George Sand
4.   Harriet Tubman
5.   Eleanor Roosevelt

F. *The roles of women in other societies*

1.   in primitive societies
2.   in Red China
3.   in modern Africa
4.   in modern Asia

G. *Women's past*

1.   women's education
2.   women's work
3.   women's social life
4.   women's entertainment

## II. Textbook Evaluation

A. *Social Studies Texts*

Examine the social studies textbooks you are using for your own classes, and look for the following:

1. the percentage of space devoted to women's roles and activities
2. the percentage of space devoted to famous women
3. the types of women included
4. the activities for which women are considered important
5. the kinds of activities considered to be feminine
6. the percentage of space devoted to women's fight for equal rights
7. the activities which are considered (or assumed) to be valuable contributions to society. Which sex is most responsible for these activities?
8. the percentage of space devoted to men, including their activities, contributions, and information about their lives. How does this compare with the space devoted to women?
9. the kinds of language used which might suggest a sexual bias in favor of one sex

After you have examined the textbooks, prepare a report about the information you have found, and consider what possible action might be taken:

1 Write a letter to the publishing company informing them of any discriminations you found. Ask the company to revise the text so that women are treated equally.
2. Recommend to the book selection committee of your school that the text no longer be used.
3. Form a committee to search for a better text and recommend its usage. If there is no better text available, ask that supplementary texts be used.

B. *Other Texts*

Examine the other texts used in your school. Keep accurate records of your findings, and prepare charts and graphs which illustrate them. These records and charts will form the basis on which you can argue for change.

1. In mathematics and science textbooks look at the kinds of problems and examples given. What percentage of these show girls involved in traditional roles such as housework, shopping, cooking, and sewing? What percentage show boys in traditional masculine roles such as playing sports, repairing automobiles, or building?

2. In English textbooks, look at the examples and illustrations given in grammar and writing texts. Again decide the percentage which show men and women or boys and girls in traditional sexual roles.

3. Look at the anthologies to discover what percentage of the writers included are women. In addition, read the introductions to see whether or not women are treated differently from men. For example, is a woman's marital status or psychological condition mentioned while a man's is not? In other words, are there any remarks or language which suggest a sexual bias?

4. Look at the supplemental texts used to discover how many are written by women and, in addition, the attitudes toward woman and her roles which are reflected.

5. In foreign language textbooks, look at the examples given and the sentences suggested for translation to see whether or not they exemplify traditional attitudes about sexual roles or sexual bias.

Prepare a report of your findings for presentation to the book selection committee:

1. Recommend that all books which are biased be replaced. If this is impossible, ask that supplemental texts be purchased so that a better balance can be achieved.

2. If biased texts must be used until new ones are available, recommend that teachers point out these biases to students and that some class time be devoted to discussing them.

3. Ask the school to formulate a policy about purchasing textbooks which are sexually biased. When they reject a text for this reason, ask that a letter be written to the publisher explaining the reasons for rejection.

### III. School Activities

Investigate the following areas and make suggestions for any needed changes.

A. *Administration*

1. Find out, for example, how many women administrators there are in the school, what responsibilities they have, whether their responsibilities are drawn along sexual lines (that is, are women only responsible for women students?), and to whom they report.
2. Recommend to the administration that more women administrators be hired, if necessary.

B. *Teachers*

1. Find out what percentage of teachers are women, what subjects they teach, and if their student loads, classes, and salaries are the same as men's. Determine how many women head academic departments. In addition, discover the school policies about maternity leaves, working pregnant women, and child care.
2. Recommend to the administration that teachers of both sexes be treated equally. If there are too few women teachers in certain subject areas, suggest that more women be hired. Encourage students to work with teachers and administrators to make certain that maternity leaves are included in medical policies and that they are treated as paid temporary illnesses or leaves. Encourage the school board to include money for child care in salaries.

C. *Courses*

1. Discover which courses are closed to women students and which are required only for women students. If men and women take gym separately, discover whether their activities, equipment, and facilities are equal. Find out which elective courses are taken primarily by one sex or the other, and try to decide why this is so. In your classrooms, discover whether or not men and women are treated differently, whether their responsibilities are the same, and whether teachers expect different behavior.

In addition, determine how much attention is given in courses to women's status.

2. Make certain that all courses are open to both sexes. If gym classes are not equal, ask the administration to change this inequity by purchasing needed equipment or improving facilities. In those classes where attitudes toward women students differ from those toward men, ask the teachers to discuss sexual attitudes with the class as a group and to have students decide upon ways of changing patterns of behavior.

D. *Social activities*

1. Find out whether there are separate clubs for men and women students and if there are what functions they serve. In co-educational clubs, discover the percentage of positions of authority held by women and the extent to which women are secretaries. Check to see how many women are members of the student government and how many hold elective offices. Find out who are the editors of the student newspaper, how many women are reporters, what assignments are given them, and what kind and how much news about women is reported.

2. Point out to the administration, the teachers, and the students any sexual bias that exists in clubs or other activities. Help develop policies which will eliminate them (for example, initiate a policy of electing a woman student government president every other year). Form a women's rights club to function as an information source to the school and a social action group.

E. *Guidance*

1. Find out the kinds of guidance available for men and women students. If there are special sessions for each sex, discover the reasons. Decide the careers women are encouraged to study. In addition, discover how much information is available to women students about jobs not traditionally considered feminine.

2. With the cooperation of the guidance office, prepare a library of information about careers which are traditionally considered masculine and encourage women students to learn about them. Collect from the Women's

Bureau, U. S. Department of Labor, pamphlets about careers open to women and information about women's status. Place these in the guidance offices. In addition, begin a women's rights section in the school library.

## IV. Community Activities

Look around your community and observe the sex roles adopted by various individuals.

1. Spend at least one day each with your mother and father, acting as their shadow. Get up when they do and follow them until they go to bed. Keep a record of what they do and the amount of time spent in each activity. For example, consider Mother:

   6:00 A.M. — get up
   6:00 – 6:15 A.M. — dress
   6:15 – 6:25 A.M. — begin coffee
   6:25 – 6:45 A.M. — awaken the rest of the family

   Pay particular attention to the evening activities which engage each parent. Using your record, determine the number of hours each parent worked during the day and the percentage of time spent in each activity.

2. Observe the children in your neighborhood, including, of course, your own brothers and sisters. The kinds of questions you might consider are: Do they play together? At what ages? What games do they play? What activities are limited to one sex? How are the girls dressed differently from the boys? On the basis of your observations, decide how the sexes are raised differently.

3. Visit a large department store. Find out which sections are devoted to men and which to women, what differences exist in clothes for men and women, what gifts are recommended for one sex rather than the other, and which toys are designated for each sex. Decide how the material goods in the store reflect cultural attitudes about the sexes.

4. Prepare a profile of women and their activities in your community. Consider, for example, the types of women's clubs in the community and the functions they perform; the position of women as workers; the number and kinds

of child care facilities available and the extent to which women are involved in them; and the number of women living in poverty or on welfare.

5. Investigate the organizations and facilities available for birth control. Consider, for example, the types of organizations involved, their aims, their location, the number of clinics available, the number of facilities located in the poorer sections of town, the fees charged and the arrangements for free services, and the educational programs available. On the basis of the information you've gathered, evaluate the organizations and grade them.

Prepare a report of your observations and consider the following actions:

1. Join a women's rights organization.
2. Begin a women's rights club or chapter in your neighborhood.
3. Organize a child care center in your neighborhood or in a poverty area.
4. Establish a free baby-sitting club which parents can call when emergencies arise. Include both men and women in the club.
5. Volunteer to work in birth control clinics.
6. Establish a speakers' bureau which will give free lectures to clubs and schools about women's rights, the status of women, laws concerning women, and birth control.
7. Establish a women's rights library which is open to those who live in your neighborhood or community. In addition, recommend that your neighborhood library branches increase the purchase of books about women's rights and devote one section of the library to it. Ask them to have a women's rights display.

## V. The Media

A. *Newspapers*

Evaluate your local newspapers. Consider the following:

1. the percentage of women working for the papers, their jobs and responsibilities, the assignments women reporters receive

2. the kinds of stories which appear on the woman's pages, the amount of news about women athletes, the extent of news about women and their rights which is reported at all, the place where it appears in the paper (that is, is it buried in the back?)
3. the content of the editorial pages, the attitudes of the columnists, and the general attitudes toward women reflected in the language used throughout and in the descriptions of individual women in news stories

Evaluate nationally-known newspapers in the same way. Compare all newspapers evaluated and grade them. Then:

1. Send a copy of your findings to the editors-in-chief, asking that they respond.
2. With other members of a club, insist that hiring and positions be in accordance with Federal regulations.
3. Write letters to the editors criticizing articles or columns which reflect a sexual bias. Encourage others to write, too.
4. Act as a news source for local papers by informing them of possible stories.
5. Begin a women's newsletter or newspaper for your community.

## B. *Magazines*

Examine magazines directed toward various audiences.

1. Prepare a report about women's magazines that indicates their major interests, the attitudes about women they reflect, and the kinds of people to whom they are directed. Be certain to look at the list of editors to see how many are women.
2. Compare these magazines with feminist magazines to find out how they are different and how they are similar.
3. Examine men's magazines to discover what attitudes about women are revealed. Compare these magazines with those you examined above. Decide how the attitudes in the magazines contradict and support each other.
4. Examine, in addition, magazines directed toward both sexes. Determine what kinds of articles seem to be the most important, who writes them, and the percentage written by women. Find out how many women are on

the editorial staff and what their positions are. On the basis of your findings, decide whether the magazine discriminates against women and how it does so.

After evaluating these magazines, consider possible community pressures on publishers:

1. Organize groups to write letters to these magazines to persuade them to include articles which reflect more broadly the range of women's interests and activities.
2. Encourage the sellers of magazines in your community to order feminist magazines for their newsstands.
3. Ask the libraries to cancel subscriptions to magazines which are offensive and to subscribe instead to ones which are not. Encourage them to order a number of feminist magazines.

## C. *Television*

The following activities will help you recognize television's tremendous influence on our concepts of women's roles.

1. Watch the local news and national evening news programs on all the stations in your area. As you do, make notes on the following: the number of anchormen for each program and their sex; the number of male and female reporters; the kinds of stories both report; which stories are traditionally considered masculine or feminine and who reports them; the staff for the programs (given at the end) and the positions women hold; the kinds of news given and how much news concerns women; the words the reporters use which express their attitudes about women. On the basis of these notes, determine for each program the percentage of women involved, the kinds and levels of positions they hold, the percentage of time devoted to news about women, and the attitudes of the programs about women. Compare the programs and rate them.
2. Watch the "prime time" programs (8:00 – 10:00 P.M.) on national television. Decide how women are presented and the attitudes toward women which are presented.
3. Watch day-time television, particularly from 9:00 to 3:00 weekdays, when husbands are usually at work and children at school. Decide what kinds of programs are

the most popular, and what conclusions about women can be drawn from these programs.

4.  Watch the soap operas presented on national television. Note the problems they bring up, the interests and occupations of the major characters of both sexes, the complications of the stories, and the way these complications are resolved. Write a word portrait of the typical American woman as presented in these programs.

5.  Watch a number of talk programs, led by both men and women. Compare and contrast them and the picture of woman they present.

6.  Watch advertisements to discover what attitudes about women are expressed, what are considered to be women's primary concerns and interests, and the intelligence of the women appearing in the advertisements. Be certain to decide which sex acts as the authority. Decide which advertisements are derogatory to women and why.

7.  Watch children's shows. Decide which sex is the more respected, what activities each sex is involved in, the differences in the ways boys and girls are treated, and the ways attitudes about sexual differences are communicated.

After viewing various shows, decide how you might influence television stations to change any discriminatory attitudes you have found:

1.  Write letters to the television stations and protest any discrimination you find. Ask the stations to reject advertisements which are derogatory to women. Insist that the hiring and position of women fulfill Federal regulations.

2.  Write to companies and protest derogatory advertisements. Encourage people to boycott products which use such advertisements.

3.  Publicize, through newsletters or articles in the local paper, programs, staffing, and advertisements which are unfair to women.

4.  If you decide that the attitude of a station is not changing despite attempts to have it do so, write the Federal Communications Commission, which licenses all television and radio stations, asking them how to present a formal complaint. Prepare the complaint.

## D. *Radio*

Evaluate the programs in the same way as you would television, For example, listen to disc jockey programs. Decide what attitude toward women is presented through the records selected.

Follow the recommendations listed under "Television" for possible corrective actions.

## E. *Films*

The following suggestions will help in evaluating and, perhaps, changing women's influence in films.

1. Investigate the subject of woman's image as presented in recent American films.
2. Investigate the subject of woman's changing image as reflected in both recent and past films.
3. Attend as many films as you can which are written, directed, produced, or photographed by women and films in which the main character is a woman. Decide how these films differ from those made by men or films in which a man is the main character.
4. Compile a list of films made by women.
5. Find out how many women are involved in the film industry in positions other than actress. In particular, find out how many are producers, directors, writers, photographers, and editors. Decide whether women are represented adequately.
6. Publicize and inform people about films made by women or concerned with issues important to women. Encourage women's groups to show and discuss them.
7. Encourage your school to order films by and about women for use both in and out of class. In addition, ask the administration to initiate an evening film series which is open to the public.

### VI. Government Activities

Study the federal and local governments. Then:

1. Make a report of the number, percentage, and positions of women in local and state government posts, including elective offices.

2.  Make a report about women in Federal positions, includ-
    ing elective offices and the highest levels of national
    government.
3.  Prepare a list of current laws in your state which relate
    to women. Include in the list the date the law first came
    into effect. Decide which of these laws are out-of-date
    and which are not in accordance with recent Federal
    legislation about sex discrimination.
4.  Poll the women in your community to find out their
    attitudes toward the Equal Rights Amendment and
    women's roles in government and their knowledge of
    current issues and laws relating to women.
5.  Compile a list of current national, state, and local laws
    concerning birth control, abortion, and child care. Find
    out whether any of these laws contradict each other.
    Decide what attitudes are reflected by these laws.
6.  Compile a list of the current laws and policies at the
    national, state, and local levels concerning women who
    are legal minors. Compare these with the laws and
    policies concerning men and decide what differences
    exist.
7.  Compile a list of laws relating to criminals. Decide how
    and in what way there are sexual differences in these
    laws.

As you review your findings, consider community actions:

1.  Form a group to work for the elimination of sexual dis-
    crimination in laws and at all levels of government.
2.  Develop an education group to inform women about
    their rights, new laws, and laws which discriminate
    against women.
3.  Through political means, encourage the national, state,
    and local governments to spend adequate funds for birth
    control facilities and education and for child care facil-
    ities.
4.  Encourage women to run for public office and volunteer
    to work in their campaigns.
5.  Run for public office yourself.

# Appendices

## Selected Readings

*Feminism, Women's Liberation, and Women's Rights*

Adams, Elsie, and Briscoe, Mary Louise, eds. *Up Against the Wall, Mother.* . . . Beverley Hills, Calif.: Glencoe Press, 1971. (An Anthology; paperback is abridged.)

Amundsen, Kirsten. *The Silenced Majority.* Englewood Cliffs, N. J.: Prentice-Hall, 1971. (Also a Spectrum paperback.)

Bird, Caroline. *Born Female.* rev. ed. New York: Simon & Schuster, 1971. (Also a Pocket Book paperback.)

Bosmajian, Hamida, and Bosmajian, Haig. *This Great Argument: The Rights of Women.* Reading, Mass.: Addison-Wesley, 1972.

Carson, Josephine. *Silent Voices: The Southern Negro Woman Today.* New York: Delacorte Press, 1969. (Also a Dell paperback.)

Cooke, Joan, Bunch-Weeks, Charlotte, and Morgan, Robin, eds. *The New Woman.* New York: Bobbs-Merrill, 1970. (An Anthology; also a Fawcett paperback.)

Cudlipp, Edythe. *Understanding Women's Liberation.* New York: Coronet Communications, 1971. (A Paperback Library edition.)

Davis, Elizabeth Gould. *The First Sex.* New York: Putnam, 1971.

DeCrow, Karen. *A Young Woman's Guide to Liberation.* New York: Bobbs-Merrill, 1971. (Also a Pegasus paperback.)

Diamonstein, Barbaralee. *Open Secrets.* New York: Viking Press, 1972.

Dreifus, Claudia. *Radical Lifestyles.* New York: Lancer Books, 1971. (paperback)

Duniway, Abigail Scott. *Path Breaking: An Autobiographical History of the Equal Suffrage Movement in Pacific Coast States.* New Introduction by Eleanor Flexner. New York: Schocken Books, 1971. (paperback)

Ellis, Julie. *Revolt of the Second Sex*. New York: Lancer Books, 1970. (paperback)

Ellmann, Mary. *Thinking About Women*. New York: Harcourt Brace Jovanovich, 1968. (Also a Harvest paperback.)

Epstein, Cynthia Fuchs, and Goode, William J., eds. *The Other Half: Roads to Women's Equality*. Englewood Cliffs, N. J.: Prentice-Hall, 1971. (An Anthology; a Spectrum paperback.)

Farber, Seymour M., and Wilson, Roger H. L., eds. *The Potential of Women*. New York: McGraw-Hill, 1963. (An Anthology; also a McGraw-Hill paperback.)

Firestone, Shulamith. *The Dialectic of Sex: The Case for Feminist Revolution*. New York: William Morrow, 1970. (Also a Bantam paperback.)

Goldberg, Lucianne, and Sakol, Jeannie. *Purr, Baby, Purr*. New York: Hawthorne Books, 1972. (Also a Pinnacle paperback.)

Goldman, Emma. *Red Emma Speaks: Selected Writings and Speeches by Emma Goldman*. Compiled and edited by Alix Kates Shulman. New York: Random House, 1972. (A Vintage paperback.)

Gould, Elsie M. *American Woman Today*. Englewood Cliffs, N. J.: Prentice-Hall, 1972. (paperback)

Hennessey, Caroline. *The Strategy of Sexual Struggle*. New York: Lancer Books, 1971. (paperback)

Herschberger, Ruth. *Adam's Rib*. New York: Pellegrini & Cudahy, 1948. (Also a Har/Row paperback.)

Hole, Judith, and Levine, Ellen. *Rebirth of Feminism*. New York: Quadrangle Books, 1971. (Also a paperback.)

Johnston, Jill. *Marmalade Me*. New York: Dutton, 1971. (Also a paperback.)

Komisar, Lucy. *The New Feminism*. New York: Warner Books, 1972. (paperback)

Kraditor, Aileen S. *Ideas of the Woman Suffrage Movement 1890 — 1920*. New York: Columbia University Press, 1965. (Also an Anchor paperback.)

Kraditor, Aileen S., ed. *Up From the Pedestal, Selected Writings in the History of American Feminism*. New York: Quadrangle Books, 1968. (paperback)

Ladner, Joyce A. *Tomorrow's Tomorrow: The Black Woman*. Garden City, New York: Doubleday, 1971. (Also an Anchor paperback.)

Lerner, Gerda. *The Grimké Sisters from South Carolina*. New York: Schocken Books, 1971. (paperback)

Lloyd, Trevor. *Suffragettes International.* New York: American Heritage Press, 1971. (paperback)

Merriam, Eve. *After Nora Slammed the Door: American Women in the 1960's: The Unfinished Revolution.* Cleveland: World Publishing, 1964.

Merriam, Eve. *Growing Up Female in America — Ten Lives.* Garden City, New York: Doubleday, 1971.

Mitchell, Juliet. *Woman's Estate.* New York: Pantheon Books, 1972.

Morgan, Elaine. *The Descent of Woman.* New York: Stein & Day, 1972.

O'Neill, William. *Everyone Was Brave: A History of Feminism in America.* New York: Quadrangle Books, 1969. (paperback)

O'Neill, William, ed. *The Woman Movement: Feminism in the United States and England.* New York: Quadrangle Books, 1971. (An Anthology; paperback.)

Parker, Gail, ed. *The Oven Birds: American Women on Womanhood,1820 — 1920.* Garden City, New York: Doubleday, 1972. (An Anthology; also an Anchor paperback.)

Ross, Pat. *Young and Female.* New York: Random House, 1972.

Roszak, Betty, and Roszak, Theodore, eds. *Masculine/Feminine.* New York: Harper & Row, 1969. (An Anthology; also a Harper Colophon paperback.)

Seaman, Barbara. *Free and Female.* New York: Coward, McCann & Geoghegan, 1972.

Stambler, Sookie, ed. *Women's Liberation, Blueprint for the Future.* New York: Charter Communications, 1970. (An Anthology; an Ace paperback.)

Sullerot, Evelyne. *Woman, Society, and Change.* Translated by Margaret S. Archer. New York: McGraw-Hill, 1971. (Also a McGraw-Hill paperback.)

Thompson, Mary Lou, ed. *Voices of the New Feminism.* Boston: Beacon Press, 1970. (An Anthology; also a paperback.)

Ware, Celestine. *Woman Power: The Movement for Women's Liberation.* New York: Tower Publications, 1970. (paperback)

Woolf, Virginia. *Three Guineas.* New York: Harcourt, Brace & World, 1938. (Also a Harbinger paperback.)

*The Social Sciences, Philosophy, and Law*

Bebel, August. *Women Under Socialism.* Introduction by Lewis A. Coser. New York: Schocken Books, 1971. (paperback)

Bettelheim, Bruno. *The Children of the Dream*. New York: Macmillan, 1969. (Also an Avon paperback.)

Commission on Population Growth and the American Future. *Population and the American Future*. New York: New American Library, 1972. (A Signet paperback; also available from the United States Government Printing Office.)

DeBenedictis, Daniel J. *Legal Rights of Married Women*. New York: Simon & Schuster, 1969. (A Cornerstone Library paperback.)

Decter, Midge. *The Liberated Woman and Other Americans*. New York: Coward, McCann & Geoghegan, 1971.

Ginzberg, Eli, *et al. Educated American Women. Life Styles and Self-Portraits*. New York: Columbia University Press, 1966. (A Columbia paperback.)

Lopata, Helena Z. *Occupation: Housewife*. New York: Oxford University Press, 1971. (Also a paperback.)

Marx, K., Engels, F., Lenin, V. I., and Stalin, J. *The Woman Question: Selections*. New York: International Publishers, 1970. (An Anthology; paperback.)

Masters, R. E. L., and Lea, Edward, eds. *The Anti-Sex: The Belief in the Natural Inferiority of Women: Studies in Male Frustration and Sexual Conflict*. New York: Julian Press, 1964. (An Anthology.)

Mead, Margaret. *Male and Female*. New York: William Morrow, 1949. (Also a Dell paperback.)

New York City Commission on Human Rights. *Women's Role in Contemporary Society*. New York: Avon Books, 1972. (paperback)

Russier, Gabrielle. *The Affair of Gabrielle Russier*. Translated by Ghislaine Boulanger. Introduction by Mavis Gallant. New York: Knopf, 1971.

Sexton, Patricia Cayo. *The Feminized Male*. New York: Random House, 1969. (Also a Vintage paperback.)

Shaw, George Bernard. *The Intelligent Woman's Guide to Socialism and Capitalism*. Garden City, N.Y.: Garden City Publishing, 1928.

Thurber, James, and White, E. B. *Is Sex Necessary?* New York: Harper & Row, 1950. (Humor; also a Dell paperback.)

Watts, Alan. *Nature, Man, and Woman*. New York: Pantheon Books, 1958. (Also a Vintage paperback.)

*Women pro & con*. Mt. Vernon, New York: Peter Pauper Press, 1958. (An Anthology)

*Autobiography and Biography*

Curie, Eve. *Madame Curie*. Translated by Vincent Sheen. Garden City, New York: Doubleday, 1937. (Also a Pocket Book paperback.)

Dahmus, Joseph. *Seven Medieval Queens*. Garden City, New York: Doubleday, 1972.

Duncan, Isadora. *My Life*. New York: Liveright, no date. (Also a University Publishers and Distributors paperback.)

Fraser, Antonia. *Mary Queen of Scots*. New York: Delacorte Press, 1969. (Also a Dell paperback.)

Lash, Joseph P. *Eleanor: The Years Alone*. New York: Norton, 1972.

McCarthy, Abigal. *Private Faces/Public Places*. Garden City, New York: Doubleday, 1972.

*Novels*

Austen, Jane. *Emma*. (Available in many editions.)

Bronte, Charlotte. *Jane Eyre*. (Available in many editions.)

Bronte, Emily. *Wuthering Heights*. (Available in many editions.)

Chopin, Kate. *The Awakening*. New York: Capricorn Books, 1964. (paperback)

Drabble, Margaret. *The Millstone*. New York: William and Company, 1965. Also a Signet paperback.)

Dreiser, Theodore. *Sister Carrie*. (Available in many editions.)

Eliot, George. *Middlemarch*. (Available in many editions.)

Flaubert, Gustave. *Madame Bovary*. (Available in many editions.)

Green, Hannah. *I Never Promised You a Rose Garden*. New York: Holt, Rinehart, & Winston, 1964. (Also a Signet paperback.)

Hardy, Thomas. *Tess of the D'Ubervilles*. (Available in many editions.)

Kaufman, Sue. *Diary of a Mad Housewife*. New York: Random House, 1967. (Also a Bantam paperback.)

Lawrence, D. H. *Women in Love*. (Available in many editions.)

Lessing, Doris. *The Golden Notebook*. New York: Simon & Schuster, 1962. (Also a Ballantine paperback.)

Orwell, George. *1984*. New York: Harcourt Brace Jovanovich, 1949. (Also a New American Library paperback.)

Plath, Sylvia. *The Bell Jar*. New York: Harper & Row, 1971. (Also a Bantam paperback.)

Roiphe, Anne Richardson. *Up the Sandbox!* New York: Simon & Schuster, 1971. (Also a Fawcett paperback.)

Shulman, Alix Kates. *Memoirs of an Ex-Prom Queen*. New York: Knopf, 1972.

*Poetry*

Millay, Edna St. Vincent. *Collected Poems*. New York: Harper & Row, 1956.
Plath, Sylvia. *Ariel*. New York: Harper & Row, 1961.
Sexton, Anne. *Transformations*. Boston: Houghton, Mifflin, 1971.

*Plays*

Aristophanes. *Lysistrata*. (Available in many editions.)
Congreve, William. *The Way of the World*. (Available in many editions.)
Euripedes. *The Trojan Women*. (Available in many editions.)
Lamb, Myrna. *The Mod Donna and Scyklon Z: Plays of Women's Liberation*. New York: Pathfinder Press, 1971. (paperback)
Shakespeare, William. *Much Ado About Nothing*. (Available in many editions.)
Shakespeare, William. *The Taming of the Shrew*. (Available in many editions.)
Strindberg, August. *Miss Julie*. (Available in many editions.)
Strindberg, August. *The Father*. (Available in many editions.)

*Short Stories*

Porter, Katharine Anne. *Collected Stories*. New York: Harcourt Brace Jovanovich, 1965.
Wasserman, Barbara Alson. *The Bold New Women*. rev. ed. New York: Fawcett, 1970. (Also a Fawcett Premier paperback.)

## Selected Feminist Magazines

*General*

*AAUW Journal*. Published seven times yearly. American Association of University Women, 2401 Virginia Avenue, NW, Washington, D. C. 20087.
*Aurora, Prism of Feminism*. Published four times yearly. Rockland County Feminists, 24 De Baun Avenue, Suffern, New York 10901.

*Battle Acts.* Published six times yearly. Women of Youth Against War and Fascism, 58 West 25th Street, New York, New York 10010.

*Black Maria.* Published four times yearly. P. O. Box 230, River Forest, Illinois 60305.

*A Journal of Female Liberation.* Published irregularly. Cell 16, 2 Brewer Street, Cambridge, Massachusetts.

*Libera.* Published three times yearly. Eshlemann Hall, University of California at Berkeley, Berkeley, California 94720.

*Notes From . . .* (In print: *the Second Year, the Third Year*): *Women's Liberation.* Published once yearly. Notes, P. O. Box AA, Old Chelsea Station, New York, New York 10011.

*Progressive Woman.* Published two times monthly. Corson Publishing Inc., P. O. Box 510, Middlebury, Indiana 46540.

*The Second Wave: A Magazine of the New Feminism.* Published four times yearly. Box 303, Kenmore Square Station, Boston, Massachusetts 02215.

*Up From Under.* Published three times yearly. 339 Lafayette Street, New York, New York 10012.

*Velvet Glove.* Published six times yearly. The Velvet Glove Press, P. O. Box 188, Livermore, California 94550.

*Women (A Journal of Liberation).* Published four times yearly. 3028 Greenmount Avenue, Baltimore, Maryland.

*Women Studies Abstracts.* Published four times yearly. P. O. Box 1, Rush, New York 14543.


*Special*

*Aphra.* Published four times yearly. Box 273, Village Station, New York, New York 10014. (Literature)

*The Feminist Art Journal.* Published four times yearly. 41 Montgomery Place, Brooklyn, New York 11215. (Art)

*Shameless Hussy Review.* Published once yearly. P. O. Box 424, San Lorenzo, California. (Art and Literature)

*The Woman's Journal.* Published four times yearly. Valley Women's Center, 200 Main Street, Northampton, Massachusetts 01060. (Art and Literature)

*Women and Film.* Published three times yearly. 2802 Arizona Avenue, Santa Monica, California 90404. (Film)

*Women's Rights Law Reporter.* Published six times yearly. 119 Fifth Avenue, New York, New York. (Law)

## Selected Films,
## Annotated

The following companies are good sources for films about women. You may wish to write for their most recent catalogues:
1. American Documentary Films, 336 West 84th Street, New York, New York 10024
2. Contemporary Films/McGraw-Hill Films: information; 1221 Avenue of the Americas, New York, N. Y. 10036; distribution; Princeton Road, Hightstown, N. J. 08520.
3. New Day Films (rents and sells only films about women), 267 West 25th Street, New York, N. Y. 10001

*Films*

*Abortion.* Women's Collective, Boston. An angry film about abortion and womens rights. (B/W, 30 min, 16 mm) Dist: American Documentary Films.

*Abortion and The Law.* C.B.S. News. Legislation and its effect in a number of countries. (B/W, 54 min, 16 mm) Dist: American Documentary Films.

*American First Ladies.* Their influence on America's traditions and customs. (color, 24 min, 16 mm) Dist: Contemporary Films/McGraw-Hill Films.

*Anything You Want To Be.* Liane Brandon. "Humorously depicts the conflicts and absurdities that beset a high school girl." (B/W, 8 min, 16 mm) Dist: New Day Films.

*A to B.* Nell Cox. The identity crisis of a sixteen year old girl. (color, 36 min, 16 mm) Dist: Nell Cox, 150 West 87th Street, New York, N. Y. 10024.

*Behind the Veil.* Eve Arnold. Documentary about harem life in Arabia. (color, 50 min, 16 mm) Dist: Richard Price Associates,, 314 West 56th Street, New York, N. Y. 10019.

*Betty Tells Her Story.* Liane Brandon. (short film) Dist: Liane Brandon, 2½ Douglass Street, Cambridge, Mass. 02139.

*Borderline.* A teen-age girl on the borderline of delinquency. (B/W, 27 min, 16 mm) Dist: Contemporary Films/McGraw-Hill Films.

*The Cabinet.* Suzanne Bauman. Dolls come to life. (color, 13 min, 16 mm) Dist: Suzanne Bauman Productions, 25 Grove Street, New York, N. Y. 10014.

*Cleo From 5 to 7.* Agnes Varda. A female singer wanders around Paris while waiting to learn the outcome of an examination for cancer. (French, B/W, 90 mins, 35 mm) Dist: Contemporary Films/McGraw-Hill Films.

*Courtship and Marriage.* Courting customs in Sicily, Iran, Canada, and India. (B/W, 60 min, 16 mm) Dist: Contemporary Films/McGraw-Hill Films.

*Cover Girl: New Face in Focus.* Frances McLaughlin Gill. A girl comes to New York City to become a model. (color, 28 min, 16 mm) Dist: FMG Productions, Inc., 49 East 86th Street, New York, N. Y. 10028.

*Dona and Gail: A Study in Friendship.* A case study of two post-high school girls in a large city who become friends because they are both lonely. (B/W, 49 min, 16 mm) Dist: Contemporary Films/McGraw-Hill Films.

*Engagement: Romance and Reality.* An engaged couple begin to really know each other. (color, 15 min, 16 mm) Dist: Contemporary Films/McGraw-Hill Films.

*Family Planning: More Than a Method.* Phyllis Chunlund Johnson. Emotional problems of family planning. (B/W, 28 min, 16 mm) Dist: Planned Parenthood, World Population, 267 West 25th Street, New York, N. Y. 10001.

*Fear Woman.* Elspeth MacDougall. Story of three Ghanaian women. (color, 27 min, 16 mm) Dist: Contemporary Films/ McGraw-Hill Films.

*The Game.* A high school boy is taunted into trying to live up to his boasting about being a seducer. (B/W, 28 min, 16 mm) Dist: Contemporary Films/McGraw-Hill Films.

*Genesis 3:16.* Maureen McCue and Lois Ann Tupper. Living on a women's commune. (B/W, 20 min, 16 mm) Dist: Lois Ann Tupper, 447 Hanover Street, Boston, Mass.

*Gertrude Stein: When This You See, Remember Me.* Perry Miller Adato. Biography of the famous American ex-patriot writer. (color, 89 min, 16 mm) Dist: Contemporary Films/McGraw-Hill Films.

*Girl in Danger.* Robert Anderson. An emotionally immature girl steals, ignores rules, and runs away. (B/W, 30 min, 16 mm) Dist: Contemporary Films/McGraw-Hill Films.

*Growing Up Female: As Six Become One.* Julia Reichert and James Klein. Documentary about "the experience of being a woman in America." (B/W, 60 min; available in two 30 minute parts, 16 mm) Dist: (1) New Day Films, (2) American Documentary Films.

*Growth, Failure and Maternal Deprivation.* Documentary showing the effects of lack of parental attention, particularly mater-

nal attention, upon young children. (B/W, 28 min, 16 mm)
Dist: Contemporary Films/McGraw-Hill Films.

*Harriet Tubman and the Underground Railroad.* Story of a great
Black woman who was born a slave, escaped, and helped
others to escape from slavery. (B/W, 54 min, 16 mm) Dist:
Contemporary Films/McGraw-Hill Films.

*Helen Keller.* The famous American woman who became blind
and deaf in childhood. (color, 15 min, 16 mm) Dist: Contemporary Films/McGraw-Hill Films.

*I Don't Know.* Penelope Spheeris. Story of a boy who wants to be
a girl and a girl who wants to be a boy. (B/W, 20 min, 16
mm) Dist: Genesis Films, Ltd., 1040 North Las Palmas, Holly-
wood, Calif.

*Inside the Ladies' Home Journal.* Janet Gardner. The day two
hundred women from the liberation movement entered the
office of the *Journal's* editor-in-chief to demand changes in the
magazine. (B/W, 15 min, 16 mm) Dist: American Documentary Films.

*It Happens To Us.* Amalie R. Rothschild. Documentary about the
experiences of women who have had abortions. (B/W, 30 min,
16 mm) Dist: New Day Films.

*Janie's Janie.* Geri Ashur. Story of a white welfare mother. (B/W,
24 min, 16 mm) Dist: Downech Films, 179 Van Buren Street,
Newark, N. J. 07107.

*The Legacy of Anne Frank.* A visual presentation of the life of a
Jewish girl who spent years in hiding from the Nazis during
World War II and finally died in a concentration camp. (color,
29 min, 16 mm) Dist: Contemporary Films/McGraw-Hill
Films.

*Loren MacIver.* Mayette Charlton. An artist and her work. (color
and B/W, 23 min, 16 mm) Dist: Film Images, 17 West 60th
Street, New York, N. Y. 10023.

*Maedchen in Uniform.* Leontine Sagan. Life in a pre-World War
II Prussian girls' school. A classic. (German, B/W, 89 min,
16 mm) Dist: Radim Films, Inc., 17 West 60th Street, New
York, N. Y.

*The Merry-Go-Round.* The relationship between a boy and a girl
with the divergent viewpoints of three well-known authorities
on sex. (B/W, 23 min, 16 mm) Dist: Contemporary Films/
McGraw-Hill Films.

*Meshes of the Afternoon.* Maya Deren and Alexander Hammid.
A womans reactions to womanhood and to her husband.

Avant-garde. A classic. (B/W, 14 min, 16 mm) Dist: Grove Press, Inc., 53 West 11th Street, New York, N. Y.

*Mothers and Daughters.* C.B.S. News. Two women discuss the ways they differ politically, socially, and morally from their mothers. (B/W, 27 min, 16 mm) Dist: American Documentary Films.

*Phoebe: Story of a Premarital Pregnancy.* The mental and emotional reactions of a teenager on the day she discovers she is pregnant. (B/W, 29 min, 16 mm) Dist: Contemporary Films/McGraw-Hill Films.

*A Place of My Own.* A girl's search for a place of her own in a crowded city apartment. (color, 11 min, 16 mm) Dist: Contemporary Films/McGraw-Hill Films.

*Radcliffe Blues.* Tony Ganz. A Radcliffe woman student discusses her radicalization. (B/W, 23 min, 16 mm) Dist: American Documentary Films.

*River Boy.* A boy and his first crush on a girl. (color, 17 min, 16 mm) Dist: Contemporary Films/McGraw-Hill Films.

*Salt of the Earth.* Herbert Biberman. Story of a strike by Mexican-Americans in a mining town, where, when the men's strike is paralyzed by a Taft-Hartley injunction, the women take over and win the strike. (B/W, 94 min, 16 mm) Dist: American Documentary Films.

*Sometimes I Wonder Who I Am.* Liane Brandon. (short film) Dist: Liane Brandon, 2½ Douglass Street, Cambridge, Mass. 02139.

*The Soviet Woman.* The life of women in Russia. (B/W, 53 min, 16 mm) Dist: Contemporary Films/McGraw-Hill Films.

*Three Lives.* Kate Millett. Three women talk about themselves and their lifestyles. (B/W, 70 min, 16 mm) Dist: Impact Films, Inc., 144 Bleecker Street, New York, N. Y.

*Until I Die.* Patricia Barey and Gloria Callaci. A woman psychiatrist works with patients with terminal illnesses. (color, 29 min, 16 mm) Dist: Video Nursing, Inc., 2834 Central Street, Evanston, Ill. 60201.

*Wanda.* Barbara Loden. A divorced working-class woman is "adopted" by a thief. (color, 106 min, 16 and 35 mm) Dist: The Keedick Lecture Bureau, Inc., 475 Fifth Avenue, New York, N. Y. 10017.

*Welfare Rights.* KPIX-TV. Documentary about the first welfare rights group which, conducted largely by black women and their children, held a four-day sit-in and hunger strike at

Oakland, California, in 1965. (B/W, 30 min, 16 mm) Dist: American Documentary Films.

*Windy Day.* John and Faith Hubley. The dreams of two girls concerning growing up. (color, 9 min, 16 mm) Dist: Radim Films, 17 West 60th Street, New York, N. Y.

*The Woman's Film.* Judy Smith, Louise Alaimo, Ellen Sorrin. A documentary in which working-class women discuss their problems in society and ways to change it. (B/W, 45 min, 16 mm) Dist: Newsreel, 322 Seventh Avenue, New York, N. Y. 10001.

*The Women Get the Vote.* The struggle of American women to be franchised. (B/W, 27 min, 16 mm) Dist: Contemporary Films/McGraw-Hill Films.

*Women on the March: The Struggle for Equal Rights.* In two parts. Part I: The struggle for the vote; Part II: Women today. (B/W, 60 min — Part I, 30 min; Part II, 30 min — 16 mm) Dist: Contemporary Films/McGraw-Hill Films.

*Woo Who? May Wilson.* Amalia R. Rothschild. A housewife from Maryland at the age of sixty moves to New York City. (color, 33 min, 16 mm) Dist: Anomaly Films, 105 Second Avenue, New York, N. Y. 10003.

## Selected National Women's Organizations

Many of the groups listed below provide information about women to their members and/or the general public. You may find it useful to inquire from them about the information which is currently available.

*Women's Organizations*

American Association of University Women. 2401 Virginia Avenue, NW, Washington, D. C. 20037.

Association for the Study of Abortion. 120 West 57th Street, New York, N. Y. 10019. (Good source of information.)

Association for Women in Psychology. 1111 Ridgewood Lane, Chapel Hill, N. C. 27514.

Association of Women in Science, c/o Dr. Anne M. Briscoe, Department of Medicine, Harlem Hospital Center, New York, N. Y. 10037.

Business and Professional Women's Foundation. 2012 Massachusetts Avenue, NW, Washington, D. C. 20036. (Good source of information.)

Comision Femenil Mexicana. 4721 East Olympic Boulevard, Los Angeles, Calif. 90022.

Commission on Continuing Education of Women, Adult Education Association, 810 18th Street, NW, Washington, D. C. 20036.

Daughters of Bilitis. DOB — New Jersey, P. O. Box 62, Fanwood, N. J. 07023. (A lesbian organization.)

Federally Employed Women. National Press Building, Suite 487, Washington, D. C. 20004.

Human Rights for Women. 1128 National Press Building, Washington, D. C. 20004. (Good source of information.)

Interstate Association of Commissions on the Status of Women. c/o Dr. Kathryn Clarenbach, University of Wisconsin, 428 Lowell Hall, 610 Langdon Street, Madison, Wis. 53706.

League of Women Voters. 1730 M Street, NW, Washington, D. C.

National Association for Repeal of Abortion Laws. 250 West 57th Street, New York, N. Y. 10019.

National Chicana Foundation. 607 East Ellingbrook Drive, Montebello, Calif. 90640.

National Committee on Household Employment. 1725 K Street, NW, Washington, D. C. 20006.

National Conference on Black Women. P. O. Box 193, Pittsburgh, Pa. 15230.

National Council of Negro Women. 1346 Connecticut Avenue, NW, Washington, D. C. 20036.

National Federation of Business and Professional Women's Clubs. 2012 Massachusetts Avenue, NW, Washington, D. C. 20036.

National Organization for Women. 1957 East 73rd Street, Chicago, Ill. 60649. (Largest feminist membership organization in the country; good source of information.)

National Welfare Rights Organization. 1424 16th Street, NW, Washington, D. C. 20036.

National Women's Political Caucus. 1302 18th Street, NW, Room 603, Washington, D. C. 20036.

Network for Economic Rights. c/o Olga Madar, United Auto Workers, Solidarity House, 8000 East Jefferson Avenue, Detroit, Mich. 48214.

Sociologists for Women in Society. 2214 West Rogers Street, Baltimore, Md. 21209.

Stewardesses for Women's Rights, P. O. Box 3235, Alexandria Va. 22302.

Third World Women's Alliance. St. Peter's Church, 346 West 20th Street, New York, N. Y. 10011.

Women's Action Alliance. 370 Lexington Avenue, New York, N. Y. 10017. (Good source of information.)

Women's Caucus, American Federation of Teachers. 1012 14th Street, Washington, D. C.

Women's Caucus, American Society of Public Administration. c/o Joan Fiss Bishop, Director of Career Services, Wellesley College, Wellesley, Mass. 02181.

Women's Caucus for Political Science. P. O. Box 9099, Pittsburgh, Pa. 15224.

Women's Caucus, National Education Association, 1201 16th Street, NW, Washington, D. C. 20036.

Women's Caucus, National Lawyers' Guild. 54 West Randolph, Room 902, Chicago, Ill. 60601.

Women's Caucus, New University Conference. 622 West Diversey Parkway, Room 403A, Chicago, Ill. 60614.

Women's Equity Action League. 610 Glenn Road, State College, Pa. 16801.

Women's International League for Peace and Freedom. U. S. Section. One North 13th Street, Philadelphia, Pa. 19107.

Women in the Historical Profession. 1369 East Hyde Park Boulevard, Apartment 310, Chicago, Ill. 60615.

Women's Legal Defense Fund. c/o Gladys Kessler, 1911 R Street, NW, Washington, D. C. 20009.

Women's Rights Project, American Civil Liberties Union, 156 Fifth Avenue, New York, N. Y.

Women Strike for Peace. 1 Union Square West, Room 408, New York, N. Y. 10003.

Young Women's Christian Association. 600 Lexington Avenue, New York. N. Y. 10022.

*Federal Agencies*

Citizens' Advisory Council on the Status of Women. Department of Labor, Room 4211, Washington, D. C. 20210. (Good source of information.)

Equal Employment Opportunity Commission. 1800 G Street, NW, Washington, D. C. 20506.

Office of Federal Contract Compliance. U. S. Department of Labor, Washington, D. C. 20210.

Wage-Hour Division, U. S. Department of Labor, Washington, D. C. 20210.

Women's Bureau, U. S. Department of Labor, Washington, D. C. 20210. (Excellent source of information.)

*Other Useful Names and Addresses*

Center for Women's Studies and Services. 4004 39th Street, San Diego, Calif. 92105. (Good for information about women's studies programs.)

International Institute of Women Studies. 1615 Myrtle Street, NW, Washington, D. C. 20012. (Good source of information about scholarly information on women.)

Know, Inc. P. O. Box 86031, Pittsburgh, Pa. 15221. (A non-profit feminist press.)

Women's History Library. 2325 Oak Street, Berkeley, Calif. 94708. (Maintains an international archive of materials on the current feminist movement.)

# Index